SHORT
NATURE
WALKS
ON LONG ISLAND

W9-AKU-471

"A series of interesting walking tours . . . that require anywhere from a half hour to two hours or more. But there's no hurry, and you can proceed at your own leisurely pace. Happy hiking."

—*Newsday*, Long Island, NY

"Walks are clearly mapped with details on what to expect from each of the 52 areas visited. If you are a birder or a hiker . . . this book will enhance your explorations."

—*Country Home/Country Gardens*

Short Nature Walks Series

SHORT NATURE WALKS
ON LONG ISLAND

Fifth Edition

by
Rodney and Priscilla Albright

edited by
Robert L. Wendt

An East Woods Book

The Globe Pequot Press

Old Saybrook, Connecticut

Photography credits: Pages xii, 4, and 58, Long Island State Park Commission; page 38, Stony Brook Community Fund; page 92, D.E. Tripp; page 144, John Hollingsworth/Department of Interior Fish and Wildlife Service; pages 118 and 162, Robert L. Wendt

Library of Congress Cataloging-in-Publication Data

Albright, Rodney.
    Short nature walks on Long Island / by Rodney and Priscilla Albright : revisions by Robert L. Wendt. — 5th ed.
        p.   cm.
    "An East Woods book."
    ISBN 1-56440-895-7
    1. Hiking—New York—Long Island—Guidebooks. 2. Long Island—(N.Y.)—Guidebooks. I. Albright, Priscilla. II. Wendt, Robert L. III. Title.
GV199.42.N652L662   1996
917.47'21—dc20   95-43039
                                                          CIP

Manufactured in the United States of America
Fifth Edition/First Printing

Contents

32 20 14
48 49
17 19 21
12 31 39 33
28 29 18 23
27 30 23 22
11 13 34
Nassau
Queens County 37 38
County 36 1
35 2

Map Legend

for maps accompanying walk descriptions

- · · — · · — ·	Preserve Boundary	▲	Viewpoint
━━━━━	Major Highway	┼┼┼┼┼┼┼	Railroad
━━━━━	Other Roads	─(25)─(37)─	State and County Routes
∷∷∷∷∷	Wood Roads		
- - - - - -	Trails	★	Parking Areas
• • • • • • •	Choice Walks	Ⓟ	Permit Parking (see page 2)
▪ ▪ ▪ ▪ ▪ ▪	Nassau–Suffolk Greenbelt Trail	W	White-Paint Blazes
+ + + + + + +	Long Island Greenbelt and Pine Barrens Trails	〰️	Lakes and Ponds

Preface to the Fifth Edition

This edition updates the information in previous versions to reflect the constant changes that impact our island environment. Some are due to the forces of nature; others stem from population pressures and related land development. In addition, information has been added to a number of the walk descriptions and maps to enhance the reader's understanding of the local scene.

It should be no surprise that financial problems have forced public and private entities to cut staffs, close facilities, and change the hours when many parks and preserves are open. A special effort has, therefore, been made to get current schedules of hours, admission charges (if any), and telephone numbers (area code 516 unless specified) for all of the walks. Don't be surprised if there are further changes.

You should know that The Nature Conservancy, through both the Long Island chapter (250 Lawrence Hill Road, Cold Spring Harbor, NY 11724; 367–3225) and the South Fork–Shelter Island chapter (3 Railroad Avenue, P.O. Box 5125, East Hampton, NY 11937; 329–7689), manages extensive preserves here. They publish guides to them that supplement and expand admirably on the limited references to them in this volume, and give details on many others. Please respect the fact that the preserves are generally small in size and established for the protection of especially sensitive species and habitats. Considerate walkers are welcome in most of them, but it would be well to understand the nature of each and to check with the conservancy before venturing in.

Even though these walk descriptions are intended to attract and please casual ramblers, birders, and botanizers, we'd be remiss not to give recognition to the contributions that organized hiking groups have made to walking on Long Island. The most prominent of these is the Long Island Greenbelt Trail Conference

(23 Deer Path Road, Central Islip, NY 17222; 360–0753). Their volunteer initiative has resulted in the opening of two major cross-island trails, the Long Island Greenbelt Trail, from Heckscher Park to Sunken Meadow Park, and the Nassau Suffolk Greenbelt Trail, from Massapequa to Cold Spring Harbor. Both follow preserves, parks, parkways, and other rights-of-way from shore to shore, mostly through woods and meadows and away from the obvious presence of suburbia. The Conference also has trail maps and guides and offers a regular program of guided hikes.

Farther east, in Suffolk, the nearly complete Pine Barrens Trail, which opens up major stretches through the unspoiled pine barrens areas both west and east of Riverhead, is being developed by the conference in conjunction with local authorities. On the south fork another group, the Southampton Trails Preservation Society (537–5203), is busy laying out and linking trails to make more accessible many of the woods and preserves out there.

A hoped-for culmination of these efforts will be the Paumanok Path, a 100-mile hiking route envisioned to extend from Rocky Point on Long Island Sound, to Montauk Point. It is based in the west on the Pine Barrens Trail and on both new and existing trails east of the Shinnecock Canal. Since the Paumanok is an all-volunteer effort and the builders are faced with relatively few public lands along the route in the east, it may be some time before all the sections are linked together. In the meantime, consult with the agencies involved for current status.

The message we wish to make clear is that these blazed, linear trail systems are as much for our readers' benefit as they are for through-hikers. They exist so that we may all gain comfortable access to more nice places to walk.

While speaking of the pine barrens, it is appropriate to mention a recent development that may have a significant impact on their future. After years of arguing and litigation over the opposing views of developers, who desired little or no additional controls over land development there, and conservationists, who want little or no development at all in the 100,000-acre pine barrens area, an agreement was finally reached in June 1995 that seems workable and generally acceptable. It provides that a 52,500-acre core area will become a forest preserve like the Catskills and Adirondacks, where development is essentially prohibited, while the peripheral lands will be open to controlled development. The basic environmental goals of preventing further loss of the once extensive pine-oak forest, of habitats for endangered plants and animals, and of watershed areas crucial for recharging our underground aquifers have been achieved. How this grand plan will work out in the face of future litigation remains to be seen, but it is clear that for our walking audience it augurs good things to come.

R.L.W.

Introduction

Walking is a pastime that can be carried out almost anywhere in city or country. Such a broad view of it, however, guarantees only to exercise your muscles. A nature walk, on the other hand, implies to us an event where exercise is secondary and the true goal is to relax and enjoy seeing and exploring new surroundings, to see more of the nonurban world and its flora and fauna. That's what we are hoping to bring you even on this busy island so close to New York City. We find that there are still many places where nature has held her own and, when man has cooperated, has prospered. We've walked here for years and recommend it.

Walking on Long Island deserves a few explanatory words, since it may be different from what you expect. It takes you into bracing air, clears your mind, and sharpens your senses. It's refreshing. You don't have to scramble up many hillsides or explore dangerous terrain. There is little need for blazes, and the only equipment needed is comfortable clothing and reasonably stout shoes. Of course, the birder mustn't fail to bring her binoculars nor the photographer his camera for there are abundant opportunities to use that kind of equipment.

Most of these places described in the pages that follow are best explored by two or three people, not groups. Also, it is usually the cars that are a problem ("where can we park legally?") As a result many towns and villages, and the counties, have taken steps to limit access (parking) to the most popular recreation areas to local residents. This applies most strongly to the beaches and, to a lesser degree, parks. These restrictions, however, are enforced only from May to October (at most), when a permit to park is often required. At other times of the year ac-

Sunrise, Montauk Point Lighthouse

cess is open, and local inquiry will tell you when and where you can park. So be attentive, quiet, and courteous—and don't litter. You'll be welcome almost everywhere.

If these admonitions seem gratuitous—and indeed they might, with all the messages we receive today about litter and pollution—you will understand our deep concern as you take a closer look at our world. For as you move about on foot, you'll be constantly aware of both the fragility and the brave tenacity of nature. And because of the enjoyment you'll get from it, you'll want to admonish others to take care, too.

When you plan your walks, recognize that you may sometimes need to alter your plans because a particular area has become inaccessible or off-limits due to storm damage. This is most likely to apply to walks on or near the beaches, but occasionally woodland trails get blocked, too. Fortunately there are many alternative walks to be found almost everywhere on the island.

A word about hazards, none of which are too threatening, but should still be noted. Keep an eye out for poison ivy, which pops up almost anywhere. Ticks, especially deer ticks, have received a lot of publicity in both Nassau and Suffolk counties because of Lyme disease. They are present in the vegetation, usually in high grass. Be sure you check for those tiny devils when you get home. The deer ticks, no bigger than the head of a pin, are easy to miss. Wearing high socks over long pants and spraying your lower limbs with insect repellent can help keep them off your skin.

This book is intended to give you seasonal walking choices. Perhaps in the height of summer you'll want to seek out the wooded, cooler places and walk the beaches when the swimmers have gone home. The towns also will be more appealing when the summer crowds have thinned.

But the fact is, taking a walk is almost always a good thing to do. If it's drizzling and overcast, it's a good day to walk; if it's cold or windy—or cold *and* windy—it's a good day to walk. Just dress appropriately. As Henry David Thoreau wrote, "When we walk, we naturally go to the fields and woods: what would become of us, if we walked only in a garden or a mall?"

The Atlantic Beaches

Long Island's best-known seashore is essentially a continuous, straight, 130-mile-long barrier beach of fine sand brought down over millennia as outwash from the two glacial moraines, Harbor Hill and Ronkonkoma, that form the forked backbone of the island. The beach sports some famous sections (Coney Island, Jones Beach, Fire Island, Montauk), some densely populated areas, some miles of true seashore wilderness, but the beach is mostly distinguished by the different features along it, some man-made, some natural.

The ten sections we've chosen to highlight draw their character more from the people who use them in summer and from the nature of the communities behind the beach than from any physical differences. Every yard of the beach is the same, every yard is different; all of it is worth visiting, exploring, and remembering, in all seasons of the year. Remember especially to visit in spring and fall when the bird migrations peak.

This brings up a necessary discussion about parking at the beaches. There are very few where parking is free year-round. State and county beaches usually have a charge for everyone from Memorial Day to Labor Day, with no restrictions the rest of the year. On the other hand, town and village beaches will usually have designated parking areas with signs saying PARKING BY PERMIT ONLY. These permits are normally available only to local residents, free or for a nominal charge. Nonresidents may be able to purchase one for a stiffer price.

The good news is that these permit restrictions are enforced only in the summer (perhaps May though October or June to September), so check locally for the exact dates. Out of season, anyone is welcome to use the beaches. You will also see, however, that most beach approach roads are liberally marked with NO PARKING signs. These are enforced all year, so be sure you end up in a "permit" lot. We have tried to identify them on the maps with the symbol Ⓟ.

Beach walks are rather hard to calibrate in terms of time and effort, though we have listed mileages in many cases. Hard sand exposed by the tide makes for fairly easy walking; soft sand above the tide line or on a sand road behind the beach can be very tiring. Since all these beach walks call for you to retrace your steps to get back to the car, it may be best to time your walks so you can use the hard sand both ways.

One other caution is in order. Remember that the dunes in back of the beach are the only barrier that prevents the ocean from washing over the top in a storm and destroying whatever is behind it. This has happened countless times in the past, and so all along the coast people are asked to keep off the dunes, except at formal crossings. This prevents harm to the beach grass that helps hold the dunes in place against erosion.

We've described these beach walks in order from west to east, like all the other parts of this book, simply to be orderly; enjoy them in any sequence!

Robert Moses State Park

Fire Island stretches 32 miles from Democrat Point on the west to Moriches Inlet on the east. This barrier island features one of the world's great beaches and has, besides seventeen small summer communities, one state park (Robert Moses), one county park (Smith Point), and a number of areas that form the bulk of the Fire Island National Seashore. U.S. Park Service visitor centers at Sailor's Haven, Watch Hill, and Smith Point provide good opportunities to learn more about this delightful area, and the main office in Patchogue is the place to turn for information (289–4810).

Robert Moses State Park is the westernmost 875 acres of Fire Island and is reachable by car across causeway and bridge, which take you over Great South Bay and Fire Island Inlet to several parking fields accommodating more than 5,000 cars. It is parkway all 49 miles from New York City; the park is open sunrise to sunset.

Since this broad, flat beach is walkable any time of year, you will never be alone hiking. It is something of an adventure, because its ready accessibility draws a wide assortment of people attracted here by the sea, the sand, the spaciousness of its open sky. But it is refreshing. Breathing air tempered by the sea, observing others reveling in the out-of-doors, and watching the sandpipers scurrying to surf's edge but wheeling away into the

air as you approach, always keeping a distance from you, you'll discover somehow time will pass more quickly than you'd imagine. So look at your watch as you leave the parking area. There is uninterrupted beach ahead for more miles than you can walk today.

From the easternmost large parking lot (labeled field 5) the distances are:

East to the lighthouse 1.4 miles
East to Kismet (first Fire Island community) 2.1 miles
East to the Sunken Forest 6.7 miles
West to Democrat Point at Fire Island Inlet 3.4 miles

The beach, known for many years as Great South Beach, is indeed great, one of the finest beaches in the world. As you visit at different seasons, you will see that it changes size and shape, is cut away in winter, flattens out in summer. Erosion brings change, as does the longshore transport of sand by currents. The lighthouse, which was built in 1856, replaced the first one built at the western tip of the island in 1825, but the inlet is now 5 miles west of the light. The Corps of Engineers keeps dredging out the ship channel that separates it from the next island to the west so Fire Island no longer actively grows westward.

For a short walk head out eastward. We clock ourselves, going for about an hour, then turn around and come back, and advise you to do the same. You will probably get to the lighthouse or a bit beyond.

Perhaps it is best, if you seek solitude, to walk here after a storm or during the rain, when most people will not venture afield. But people flock together, and groups thin out as you go eastward.

There are refreshment stands, picnic shelters, and a bathhouse open in season. Field 5 is open all year and has a $4.00 parking fee. Field 2 is also open all year, but only has the $4.00 fee in the summer season. Questions? Call 669–0449.

SUNKEN FOREST

To Patchogue

Ferry

Ferry

Watch Hill

Davis Park

GREAT SOUTH BAY

Ferry

Water Island

Ferry

Fire Island Pines

To Sayville

Cherry Grove

Ferry

ATLANTIC OCEAN

Sailor's Haven

Ocean Beach

Ferry

Sunken Forest

N

Miles

0   1   2

2

Sailor's Haven
and Sunken Forest

The waves of the great Atlantic Ocean, set in motion 600 or more miles offshore by the wind, head westward unimpeded, slide up over the continental shelf, and, with almost hourly changes of mood, strike the Long Island south shore beaches with pulsations of fascinating and hypnotic qualities. Their visual aspects change too, so frequently in fact that there is never a dull day at the beach. There is never the threat of oppressive crowds. It is glorious. There is a fascination that nothing can quite describe, drawing you back again and again, refreshing you—and quietly luring you into spending an hour or a day longer than you had in mind.

We have come in the early spring, starting off in weather so thick we could not see Fire Island from the Sayville side, to have the sun later break through to show off the carpet of beach heather climbing these dunes, golden in bloom.

As the barrier beach built up, collecting more and more sand, the wind piled it up and formed these dunes. While some are only 4 or 5 feet high, many, as these here, reach a height of 35 or 40 feet.

Behind the dunes, between Cherry Grove and Point O' Woods, is a sanctuary well worth a visit that affords a pleasant walk. The Sunken Forest comprises almost forty acres of land. It is a short walk, close to Sailor's Haven ferry dock. As you cross to the south and climb the ramps protecting the dunes, you rise 35 feet above sea level and look across the top of the dunes to the Great South Bay beyond.

The dense vegetation between you and the bay is the top of the forest. Now rare, although there have been many similar forests in New Jersey as well as Cape Cod, the Sunken Forest of Fire Island has fortunately been preserved, and we are able to see here many trees that are estimated to be at least a hundred years old. The principal trees are American holly, shadblow, and sassafras, grown to a height of 35 to 40 feet. Normally these species do not reach this size because they are crowded out by stronger, taller growing trees. Here, however, the red maple, red cedar, black and post oak, and pitch pine are themselves sheared off by the salty winds from the ocean and thus all are stunted to the protecting screen height of the dunes. It is dense with the tangles of wild grape, catbrier, a floor of ferns, Canada mayflower, and false Solomon's seal. Oh yes, there's poison ivy too!

Descending the broad path into this primitive forest, you have an unusual experience similar to being in a jungle and interesting too because of the land birds. The boardwalk comes out on the bay side into almost blinding light if it is a bright day, through thickets of plume grass, hugs the sandy shore, and reenters the forest to the west, twining back through the area. On a hot summer day it's pleasantly cool.

To reach Sailor's Haven, take the ferry from River Road, Sayville. From May to November it usually operates on a regular schedule. After the summer season, service ends to Sailor's Haven but continues all winter, on a limited basis from Sayville to Cherry Grove and Fire Island Pines, which are 1 or 2 miles away on foot. Another option is to take the Ocean Beach ferry from Bay Shore—with a 3-mile walk. Call the ferries for schedules: 589–0810 in Sayville, 665–3600 in Bay Shore.

3

Smith Point West

The beach accessible at Smith Point West is one of our favorite places to walk, and the 7-mile stretch westward to Watch Hill is presently the only National Wilderness in New York State and consequently is not open to vehicles (although specially permitted four-wheel-drive vehicles may drive on the ocean beach only). A causeway and bridge lead to the eastern end of the island, where there's ample parking ($5.00 parking fee in summer months). This is at the south end of the William Floyd Parkway. Train service on the Montauk line goes to Shirley Station, 2.5 miles from the bridge.

A two-story octagonal visitor center on the dunes houses the National Seashore ranger's office (281–3010), which is open year-round and contains an informative display on beach life. Rangers may be available to guide interesting short walks from here in the summer.

The beach westward offers a walk stretchable as far as you'll be able to go. We usually head for the Old Inlet, which is about a 2-mile round trip. The National Seashore maintains a shower–rest room building there during the summer and an ocean-to-bay boardwalk as well as a small dock with a buoy-marked channel leading to it. In moderate or cold weather it's nice to come back on the sand trail (formerly used as a road) that runs inland parallel to the ocean.

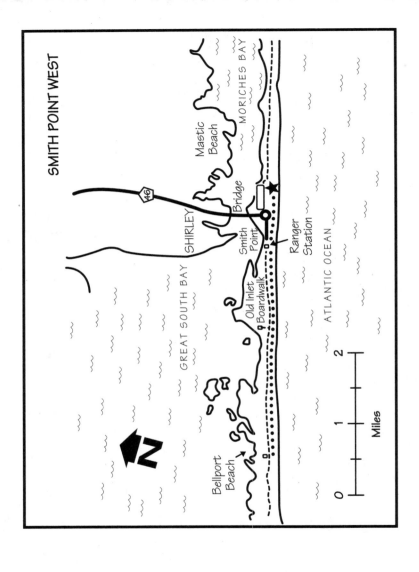

SMITH POINT WEST

GREAT SOUTH BAY

SHIRLEY

Mastic Beach

MORICHES BAY

Bridge

Smith Point

Old Inlet Boardwalk

Bellport Beach

Ranger Station

ATLANTIC OCEAN

N

0   1   2

Miles

At low tide pebbles are exposed which, in their wet state, may get you started on a pebble collection! There are white ones and black, red ones and brown, lavender, and with subtle variations, a seemingly limitless selection. In fact, that's where all the sand comes from—the rocks and stones beat against each other, reducing themselves into smaller and smaller pieces, sand being the smallest particles to which they are ever reduced. Scoop up these dry sands and, as they run through your fingers, investigate them carefully. At least half the sand is quartz, but there is hornblende, rutile, feldspar, augite, magnetite, ilmenite—a variety of names to confound you or just possibly to start you exploring a whole new world of minerals and rock. Below Hatteras, down into the beaches of the south, much of the sand is made up of tiny shell fragments, but not here on Long Island. Shells are relatively scarce. The rocks that make up these beaches were brought by the mighty glaciers of the Ice Age all the way from Canada. So as you inspect the debris of the sand, you might find anything. They tell us specks of ruby and emerald exist here— but rarely! However, if you search, you'll certainly find garnet, and the black patches contain magnetite, an important iron ore that sometimes becomes magnetized; when it does, it's called lodestone. If you run a magnet through this, you'll find particles will cling.

With no people living on this thin stretch of the barrier beach, a walk here exposes some of the fragile links in the chain of life. For among the variety of life zones—the tidal edge of the sea, the beach itself, behind the sandy swales of the dunes, and in the wetlands along the Great South Bay—is a busy world to capture your interest and excite your imagination. We see hoofprints of deer here often, but deer are remarkable in becoming invisible. Only once or twice have we actually seen them here, and then what a thrill!

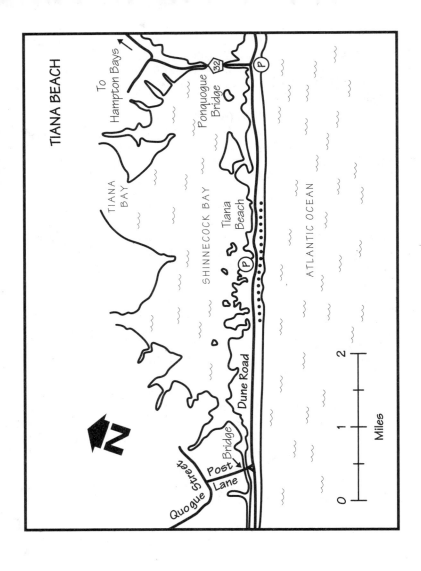

TIANA BEACH

N

To Hampton Bays

Ponquogue Bridge

32

P

TIANA BAY

SHINNECOCK BAY

Tiana Beach

P

ATLANTIC OCEAN

Dune Road

Post Bridge

Quogue Street

Lane

0   1   2

Miles

Quogue and Tiana Beaches

Cross the bridge at Quogue or Hampton Bays onto Dune Road. About midway between the two is Tiana Beach, where there's parking and easy access across the dunes.

Wide and open, the beach here is strung out with cottages all along behind the dunes, but not dominating the landscape. We generally walk a mile west, by the round apartment complex and several summer places to the Quogue Public Beach, and return. Then we walk another mile east to total an hour and a half or two hours of elapsed time. It is never too crowded.

Low tide is the best time to walk on the beach because the wet sand is compacted and settled by the waves, so all along the water's edge the firm walkway is hard enough not to hold you back in your own footsteps. Actually, water still remains between the individual grains of sand, and even on the hottest days the sun only dries the surface. There's a microscopic world of channels and ponds teeming with almost invisible life. Just watch the tiny sandpipers scurrying up to the water's edge, pecking away into the oozing sand. That's what they're after.

Quite apart from our walks, however, another reason compels us to come back here. That is Dune Road. The variety of shore birds using the wetlands along the north of the road is almost endless. Almost all these creatures who nest or visit Long Island can be seen at some spot along here, wading in the shallows, standing in the grass, or winging low over the water. During the migratory season you will see one or two dunlin, black-bellied plover, ruddy turnstone, and then another and another, until you realize that the grass or shoreline is alive with them.

Come equipped with glasses and your bird guide. You'll find your car a perfect blind from which to observe. Drive along slowly. We've seen and heard the clapper rail, with his raucous call, and watched the bittern slowly swaying as he holds his bill in the air pretending to be a reed, trying to elude us. And we have watched black skimmer after black skimmer feeding, with their precision glide along the water. You'll see it all on Dune Road.

The slimy wetlands swarm with insects, and the water is unfit to drink. But acre for acre, the salt marsh will produce more plants than any farm, fertilizing itself, needing no help from man in planting or harvesting. Not only is it the feeding ground for the migrating birds you see along Dune Road, but it provides shelter and food for small mammals as well. We've watched the muskrat swimming here and working in the shallows, for example. And the tiny fish that swim and breed here are carried out on tides to feed still larger fish miles from shore. When you see the fill on some of this wetland, you realize that environmentalists do not always win the continuing battle with developers.

5

Southampton Beach

From the Shinnecock Inlet in Southampton eastward, the beach stretches in a broad unbroken swath for 11 miles to Sagaponack Pond. In summer this area attracts, for the most part, those who are content to lie out in the sun, dip in the magnificent surf—sometimes it's too magnificent and must be respected—and picnic or fling the Frisbee. Off-season it is almost completely uninhabited except for the occasional dog walker, surf fisherman, or bird-watcher.

There are many places of public access where you may park. Sometimes there is a fee, or a parking permit is required (obtained at the Southampton Village or one of the town halls or at the beach). Out of season, however, there is no problem.

This stretch is characterized by high dunes; rather large summer houses, usually set well behind the dunes for protection; a number of guarded beaches for swimming; good walking at low tide; and many ponds just behind the dunes, where there is always more to be seen than a bird. At the east end of Shinnecock Bay, the beach ceases to be a barrier island (or here a peninsula) and all the rest of the way to Montauk becomes part of the mainland. These are classic beaches, the kind you see in marvelous color prints, the dunes covered with pale chartreuse grasses and over the broad stretches of white sand, a mist of salt spray, the sun catching the movement of the waves.

SOUTHAMPTON BEACH

At the Shinnecock or western end of this stretch there are no buildings at all, and the dunes are unusually high. Terns must nest here, for once in the spring they literally dive-bombed us. Parking out here is informal. The road peters out, so be careful unless you have a four-wheel-drive vehicle. The walk to the jetty is about 2 miles.

There are three or four other accesses to the beach. Our favorite section to walk is the one locally known as Fowlers. The approach to the high dunes is past a couple of ponds through broad potato fields, some seasons planted to wheat for rotation. The parking is in a lot off the road just before the dunes, so your walk is first to get to the beach. There are usually interesting birds on both sides of the ponds, and in August they are surrounded by huge pink or rose flowers of the marsh mallow. We turn left as we come onto the beach, walk along the water to Mecox Bay and back, making a total distance of just over 3 miles.

Beach walks clear your mind of many things. Often personal problems are replaced by other thoughts such as those stemming from the fact that geologists say these beaches are a million years old!

For a change of scene while in Southampton, it might be interesting to visit the Dupont Nature Sanctuary, at the southeast end of Captains Neck Lane. It harbors a true salt-marsh ecosystem that forms a kind of natural barrier between ocean and land. It provides a resilient buffer against the forces of storm and tide, but most importantly, it represents the first link in the food chain. This is where organic matter decays to feed even larger organisms, from plankton to fish to people.

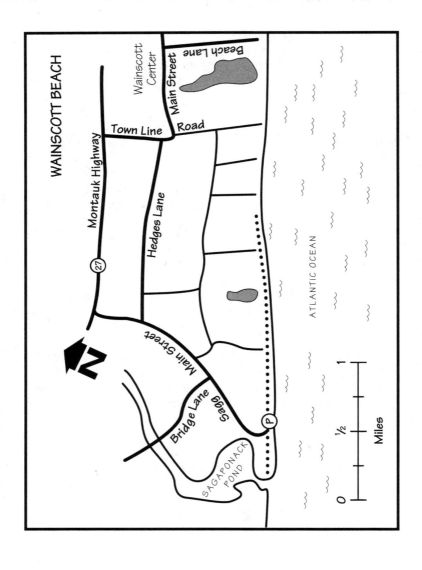

6

Wainscott Beach

Of the five unbroken stretches of beach along Long Island's south shore, Wainscott Beach, 3.6 miles from end to end, is the shortest. Many walkers have a compulsion to cover every mile of a stretch, just because it is there, and it's easy to understand the urge because there is a satisfaction to having traversed any stretch. Still, on the broad, flat strands of the coastline here, there isn't a startling surprise of discovery. One beach is very much like another. There are differences, of course, but these differences are subtle, sometimes more metaphysical than real. And since, from hour to hour, aspects of the beach walking experience change anyway, it can be misleading to describe any of Long Island's beaches in specific detail. Wainscott Beach is probably the most out-of-the-way. There are cottages all along, well back in grassy stretches. The dunes are lower. For some reason driftwood does not accumulate here to the extent it does farther east. Freighters at sea seem farther out.

To reach Wainscott Beach, turn south from the Montauk Highway 1.3 miles east of Bridgehampton on Sagg Main Street to Sagaponack, and on to the end; or go to the end of Beach Lane in Wainscott.

It's a good idea to check the tide tables before you start off and to try to do your principal walking during low tide, when the footing is more solid and the walking easier! Up on the higher ground the surface sand does dry to a greater depth, and walking becomes more laborious.

When you stand on the beach facing the sea, you can notice from many little indicators that the water pulls to the west. For the longest time we simply couldn't understand this. We'd say that the Gulf Stream was out there moving eastward and northward along the coast, so how could the water here along shore move as it obviously does, in the opposite direction? Have you asked yourself this question? Have you seen how the sand moves west with the currents, how pieces of driftwood move back toward New York? In a word, the answer is friction. The Gulf Stream is a very large river, about 40 miles wide and 2,000 feet deep, with a volume of water a thousand times larger than our biggest river, and it moves about 5.5 miles per hour in a northeasterly direction. As it moves, the water along the shore is set into counter-currents and eddies that flow for a time in the reverse direction because of the friction of the shore.

7

East Hampton Beach

From Georgica Pond the Long Island South Beach is uninterrupted for 22.2 miles to Montauk. Locally the stretch is referred to as East Hampton Beach, Amagansett Beach, Napeague Beach, or Montauk Beach, depending on its proximity to the adjoining community. The entire stretch is magnificent and eminently walkable.

Parking on East Hampton beaches is restricted to residents only during the season. East Hampton is chic, as a town, beautifully maintained, and handsome because of tree-shaded lanes and many attractive houses. It has a casual dignity and considerable local civic pride. We've driven along streets here early in the morning, before breakfast, on the way to the beach and seen golden pheasant, one after another, strutting across village greenswards. This pastoral, relaxed village atmosphere is the secret of East Hampton's jealously guarded charm, and a strong effort is being made to keep it this way.

A good walk on the East Hampton Beach is from the village beach east of Hook Pond; walk westward to the Georgica Pond inlet and return. The total distance, round-trip, is 6.4 miles. On your right as you head out will be the Maidstone Golf Club and Hook Pond, which is a good birding area. Beyond Main Street Beach the dune area is fairly primitive, low and windswept. Off-season you can find a place to park.

EAST HAMPTON BEACH

EAST HAMPTON

Dunemere Lane

114

27

Montauk Highway

Georgica Road

Lily Pond Lane

Ocean Avenue

Maidstone Golf Club

HOOK POND

GEORGICA POND

ATLANTIC OCEAN

Miles

0   ½   1

The beach here is in striking contrast to, say, the beaches west of Jones Beach, where our urban sprawl has crowded out the dunes. The charm and attractiveness of Eastern Long Island is threatened by growth—the statistically predictable population explosion and overcrowding that seem inevitable. East Hampton is vigorously trying to preserve its heritage, limit its growth, save its open land for living space. As you walk Long Island, you will appreciate its openness, see the need to save its wild areas, but feel the pressures crowding in to crush its rural character. You may feel yourself helpless as an individual in a crowded society and may ask yourself what you can do to help in conserving this. The answer seems to be to become involved, to work with others, such as The Nature Conservancy, for a common end. The administration of our civic affairs apparently works under pressure of an aroused citizenry.

AMAGANSETT BEACH

8

Amagansett Beach

An easy direct access to Amagansett Beach is to turn south off the Montauk Highway on Indian Wells Highway (2.5 miles east of East Hampton, but before you reach Amagansett). At its end is a bathhouse on the east side, and opposite this, Sheppard's Dunes, an eight-acre area acquired and protected by The Nature Conservancy to preserve its natural state. Parking during the season is reserved for residents. It's better to walk in late spring or early fall anyway.

The beach itself has character. Houses sit almost half a mile up from the beach on bluffs overlooking the sea, and the dunes are wild. So our suggestion is to walk to Maidstone Golf Club, which is 2.5 miles to the west on the wide beach, then return.

For anyone who has lived in inland wooded areas, the plants and ground cover of the seashore offer a fascinating world of discovery. When there's a break in the dunes, as there is here, you can be tempted to cross in order to examine interior plant life. But don't do it. You will crush the dune grasses, making the passage vulnerable to wind erosion. And just one such spot can actually weaken an entire dune. So be conservation minded and alert to damage to any plant life. You will be able to find a path allowing you to observe.

The beach grass, with its long, curving leaves, is the principal stabilizer for the dunes. It gets its nourishment from wind-blown minerals, grows up, sends its roots deep, follows the contours of the dunes. The false heather is another, with bright buttery yellow blossoms from May through July. It is a low, shrubby plant adapted to life on the shifting sands.

Just over the dunes, when there's soil enough, the beach pea will take hold, send its vinelike leaflets swarming, the ends with little tendrils like a pig's tail. You will want to examine the pea flowers, which are delicate in shades of violet and purple, blossoming throughout the summer. Inland, thickets of beach plum and bayberry take hold with beautiful fruit in the fall.

When the dunes are stabilized, it is amazing the exuberance that nature displays. Above all, you should beware the poison ivy, rampant near the beach. You will find rugosa rose, seaside goldenrod, thistle, and blueberry. It is really quite startling to realize the wide variety there is in plant life near the beach.

9

Napeague Beach

After you leave Amagansett, driving east, the ocean comes into view from the highway for the first time. The peninsula abruptly narrows; two bodies of water—Napeague Bay and Harbor—extend southward, making the land here less than a mile wide until you reach Hither Hills (about 6 miles). The road parallels the ocean about a half mile inland. The land is flat with low dunes and familiar seaside plants. Napeague Beach extends eastward from Amagansett. It's easiest to get onto the beach through the Hither Hills State Park.

Out here is a good place to get a feeling for the forces that shaped Long Island's topographical features. As you leave Amagansett you see the high dunes petering out, then at Hither Hills the land mass piles up again, now in contours and hills that are more than 150 feet above sea level. The land masses are the result of the swath pushed and dumped here by the glaciers, and the beaches, from the continuous action ever since of wind and sea. Great rolling breakers have been moving in on the Long Island shoreline for a million years since the first glacier came down and for more than 25,000 years since the last, scooping up rocks and sand, rubbing and grinding and depositing the fine, fine particles, forming the present continuous beach. And wind has blown it around. What with storms and tides and long-shore transit of sands by currents, there have been constant

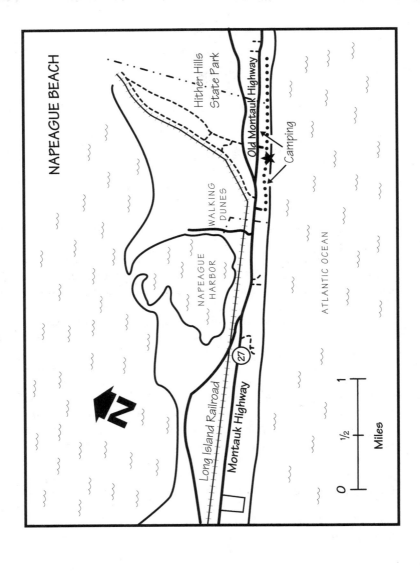

NAPEAGUE BEACH

Hither Hills
State Park

Old Montauk Highway

Camping

WALKING
DUNES

NAPEAGUE
HARBOR

ATLANTIC OCEAN

N

Long Island Railroad

Montauk Highway

27

0   ½   1

Miles

changes in elevations and shorelines. It is recorded that there were seven inlets east of Fire Island in 1743—but then Fire Island was 55 miles long. It was not until 1931 that big waves and high tides separated the dunes and broke through Fire Island at Moriches Inlet in a destructive storm. And it is inevitable that there will be further change.

As you walk the Napeague Beach, go east for a time and see the high bluffs where the Ronkonkoma Moraine comes right to the sea. Turn around and walk past the park to the low dunes. Along the way you will surely see a fisherman or two.

Offshore the bottom is even and shoals quite gradually, and you will generally see commercial and sport fishing boats trolling along here as the fishing is apt to be good. At least surfcasters have this attitude. During the summer there are schools of bluefish, sea bass, porgies, and flounder. Late in the autumn striped bass can be caught and, through the winter, cod.

10

Montauk Beach

There's a gap in the morainal hills that defines Montauk Beach, about a 3.5-mile stretch of broad sandy beach from the high dunes along the Old Montauk Highway. East of this you come to the 70-foot-high bluffs, a kind of land's end, halfway between New York City and the farthest reach of Cape Cod, which is Montauk Point. Kirk Park Beach, right in town, is a popular spot all year, since access is easy and the beach is nice and wide. There will be bathers and people lying in the sun if it's summer. And if you walk west toward the dunes, you should surely see surfers in wet suits, because the conditions are evidently good there.

For a less busy area with bluffs you can walk on about a mile east on Route 27 and turn down Ditch Plains Road to reach the town beach there. It's a fine, wide strand too, but if you head west on footpaths just in back of the low bluff, you'll soon be high enough for dramatic views of the beach below, the higher bluffs east to Montauk Point, and, close at hand, a few of the long, overgrown "buildings" that were gun emplacements for coastal defense during World War II.

The best surfing waves are known as spilling breakers—those that, as they approach the beach, have a line of foam spilling down their front, always just about to break but holding off for quite a while. Since the more gradual the slope of the bottom, the longer the wave will hold off breaking, it stands that the best surfing is on that kind of beach that has a long stretch underwater with almost no slope at all.

There is never a day on these waters when there is no surf whatsoever, though it is possible for it to be too dull for those who make a sport of it. The whole science of waves is complex, but it is interesting to know that a wave will break when the ratio of the height of the wave to the depth of water is about three to four; that is to say that a 6-foot wave will break in about 8 feet of water.

The wave action is caused principally by the wind's force against the surface of the water. The water itself actually moves very little. You can see this when you watch a cork or piece of driftwood bobbing at sea; after the wave has passed, you see how little the cork has moved. When a wave passes through very shallow waters, it lifts and stirs up sand from the bottom, so the loose grains of sand settle in a place different from where they started. That's how waves change and shape the contours of beaches.

The changes in the beach would not, most likely, startle the Montauk Indians, whose name it bears. The Montauks, who were so naturally protected here from their mainland enemies, made quantities of wampum on these beaches from the shells of periwinkles and quahogs. No, these changes would not startle them half as much as the changes on land, where the indigenous hardwoods of New England—beech, oak, and maple—and the 140- or 150-foot tulip trees from which they fashioned their canoes have all been destroyed.

Towns to Explore on Foot

One of the joys of walking is to step out of the fetters of time, to while away and unwind at a leisurely pace and with a certain detachment. Keeping alert to the surroundings in this carefree state, you'll experience a feeling of satisfaction. Walking along the edge of the sea may give you a sense of leaping back in time, and walking along narrow streets of an old village may make you feel nostalgic, feeding your hankering for a simpler life.

Long Island was colonized by New Englanders, mostly from Connecticut, and English architectural influences are visible in a number of places, some dating as far back as the Old House in Cutchogue (1649). There are Dutch influences, too, which pushed eastward from New Amsterdam.

Rural village charms that still exist on Long Island are mainly left over from the nineteenth century. By then the settlements had established a character that has strong appeal to us today. There are other communities you might want to explore besides the six we describe here. They offer interesting architecture and still retain vestiges of rural village charms. We suggest you try to investigate *Amityville,* south of Farmingdale at the end of Broad Hollow Road and south of the Sunrise Highway; *Roslyn Park,* just south of North Hempstead Turnpike between Port Washington Boulevard and Glen Cove Road; and the hamlet of *Oyster Bay,* all in Nassau County. And in Suffolk County, visit *Cold Spring Harbor,* on North Hempstead Turnpike 2 miles west of Huntington and *Northport* east of Huntington and Centerport, north of Route 25A. There's an old pre-Revolutionary church on Main Street at the Setauket Green in *Setauket,* west and north of Port Jefferson. And *Riverhead* offers a good many places to explore.

DOUGLAS MANOR

1

½

0
Miles

LITTLE
NECK
BAY

N

Udall's Cove
Preserve

L.I.R.R.

Shore Road

Marinette Street

Douglas Road

West Drive

Hillside Avenue

36th Avenue

Cross Island Parkway

Douglaston
R.R. Station

Douglaston Parkway

Boulevard

25A Northern

Douglas Manor

Douglas Manor is a community of cozy-looking houses set on a peninsula that juts into Little Neck Bay at the eastern end of Queens County. It is that part of Douglaston that lies entirely north of the tracks of the Port Washington Branch of the Long Island Rail Road, and we think you would really enjoy the walk around the peninsula, along a sidewalk by the water's edge much of the way. If you come by train, get off at the Douglaston station. By car, leave Northern Boulevard on Douglaston Parkway and head north past the station area until you find a place to park. That may be several blocks during the week, when commuters are here in numbers.

Start your walk on the west side by going down 36th Avenue to the shore road and then heading north along Little Neck Bay. In the summer this is a very popular place for shore birds and modest sailboats. The waters are unusually clean, largely due to the total absence of commercial activities and marinas. Once you round the north point and head down Marinette Street and Douglas Road, you'll be on the edge of a small park and a large, marshy wildlife preserve that extends over to the far shore. To return to your starting point from the end of Douglas Road, just turn right on Hillside Avenue and continue over the hill to West Drive. The total walking distance, starting at the station, is about 2.5 mostly level miles.

If you take the additional time to expore the streets of Douglas Manor, which we reccommend, you will quickly sense that it is an unusual community. Although there are a few old houses, one dating to 1732, the town's history dates from around 1906, when it became a genteel housing development. The 535 houses now encompass almost every conceivable style of architecture, and range from virtual cottages to mansions. Many enjoy fine water views.

There has always been a strong bent here for community improvement, as evidenced by the fact that it has the largest community garden club in New York State. In another sense it is nearly an arboretum, as over the years a continuing theme has been the introduction of well over one hundred varieties of trees. The streets are graced by innumerable giants, topped by a 500-year-old white oak on Arleigh Road. Many rare and exotic varieties are also to be found.

All in all there is much to catch your eye here—not only the water traffic one would expect on the sound and in the bay, but also the wildlife, which is abundant for so densely populated a county.

12

Sea Cliff

"The style of the houses in Sea Cliff," says one local resident with a measure of civic pride, "is what we call 'Carpenter Gothic.'" Perhaps this sets in your mind's eye a village that is a collection of highly individual gingerbread houses on which personal effort has been applied over the years. Actually there's an ample supply of larger, well-maintained Victorian ones as well, not to mention a real diversity in more modern varieties. You should enjoy a walk in Sea Cliff for surprises! It rolls comfortably over high bluffs overlooking Hempstead Harbor. Narrow streets running up and down steep slopes, some very small parcels of land, and loving care are the complementary parts that make up a whole picture of Sea Cliff that forms as you trudge around the town on foot.

Start off by parking near Clifton Park and walk along westward on Sea Cliff Avenue. There are some big houses here, and you'll cross through the business district, perhaps quickly sensing that the principal industry is selling antiques these days. When you reach Central Avenue, detour briefly around to the north side of the Village Hall (former Methodist Church) to visit the Sea Cliff Museum. It is the community's response to the unique historical background of the town and has interesting artifacts and photographs from the past. There is also an interesting booklet to be had, "This is Sea Cliff," which describes the background of the village, the many parks, and the other points of interest. It costs $2.00, and it can also be bought in the Village

Hall during normal business hours. Hours for the museum are Saturday and Sunday from 2:00 to 5:00 P.M. (January and February from 2:00 to 4:00 P.M.), closed in August. For more information call 671–0090.

Return to Sea Cliff Avenue and continue on it. Shortly you will reach Memorial Park, site of an old inn, which was seized and demolished by the town for back taxes. The property is on the heights, and you will come upon a grand view of Long Island Sound.

Walk north on Prospect Avenue, left down Cliffway, and north again on The Boulevard. Two sets of steps will bring you back up to Prospect. An alternate longer walk is to go from Memorial Park down Prospect Avenue to the shoreline and follow it south as it curves along under the lovely old plane trees (sycamores) to Scudders Pond. Returning, you can explore the narrow streets along Sea Cliff's "Cliff Side" by following Littleworth Lane back up to Carpenter, thence along it to Glen Avenue and the park.

The first gathering of people here was really a Methodist summer camp meeting with tents, picnics, and summer smiles on faces of earnest city folk, singing hymns on the wooded hills above the water, away from the ruffians of the city. That was in 1865. Good steamboat service to New York City was available and convenient from the pier in the harbor. They later bought 240 acres from the Carpenter family, who owned the farmlands, and divided it. The atmosphere was so congenial that people eventually built little houses on their 40-by-60-foot lots to make the camp more permanent and lavished every spare dollar they could to make it attractive.

By 1895, however, word of its charms having spread, it had become a very popular summer resort, and many large Victorian houses had been built. There was a cable car up the cliff, and a boardwalk had been built along the shorefront. The Long Island Rail Road was running trains into the little gingerbread station on a regular schedule, spring, summer, and fall, and there were four boats daily between Sea Cliff and New York. Today it stands as one of the best-preserved little square miles around.

OLD BETHPAGE VILLAGE

N

Parking ★

Visitor Center

Fairgrounds

Store

Church

Inn

School

Black-smith

Powell Farm

POND

Miles

0    $\frac{1}{10}$ $\frac{2}{10}$

13

Old Bethpage Village

Unlike the other communities, Old Bethpage Village is a restoration, a composite made up of simple houses and shops with some architectural merit, regrouped here on a 200-acre site ample enough to provide a proper setting for the buildings and re-create the atmosphere of a mid-nineteenth-century village. And it is a pleasant surprise. We think it makes a delightful walk, a lovely switch in centuries.

You will find a parking lot and a reception center of contemporary design. Here there are an adequate cafeteria, an excellent gift shop, and a small auditorium showing a film on the restoration. A $5.00 admission fee is charged, with reductions for senior citizens and children. Allow a couple of hours and spend another if you can make the time.

We walked into the days before the mechanization of the farm. This illusion is skillfully achieved. The dirt path we followed is bordered by a post-and-rail fence; the field through which it ambled lay fallow, but liberally sprinkled with Queen Anne's lace and butterflies. Birds chirped. There was the faint, not unpleasant, organic smell that emanates from a farmyard.

We were greeted at one of the houses by an eager youth who showed us through. It had been a bayman's dwelling. Uncluttered, simply furnished, it set an informal, friendly air to our visit. Altogether forty-five buildings, all original structures, have been saved from destruction and moved here to form a charming nineteenth-century village.

At the crossroads is a general store, with the proprietor's living quarters under the same roof, an inn serving root beer in the Tap Room, and a blacksmith's forge. By this time we had noticed that all the guides were dressed in clothes of the period. It is not correct to say that they were wearing costumes—the garb is simple, functional, and doesn't at first catch your eye.

The Powell farm is functioning. There are pigs and cows, chickens and geese. The ladies were baking bread, and a pot of soup hung simmering from the crane over coals smoldering away in the fireplace. It was vegetable soup, and the gardens had provided all the ingredients. The flies buzzed, a Canada goose honked, and the old sow lay sprawled out in the mud.

It is an uncluttered, friendly, helpful little valley, and the attitudes of all the people working here make it so.

The walk around the loop is 1.5 miles. During the school year we were told there are daily groups—so our suggestion is to come, as we did, on a summer's day. Let the natural breezes provide the stream to float your daydreams on. Lengthen your stride, but slow down your pace, and reflect how downright simple the necessities of life can be. The 1.5-mile walk plus the other exploring footsteps will add up to enough on a hot afternoon.

Remember, though, that the village is open and alive all year (except in January and February), with daily hours from 10:00 A.M. to 5:00 P.M.; so it is possible to experience a variety of activities having to do with the passing of the seasons. For specific schedules and information, call 572–8400.

The enterance to the village is on the east side of Round Swamp Road, about one mile south of the Long Island Expressway (Route 495), exit 48.

14

Stony Brook

Because Stony Brook is old and handsome, we think you should see it for its unique charm and Long Island bayside country atmosphere.

The focus for visitor interest here is the complex of buildings now known as The Museums at Stony Brook. Founded in the 1930s, the museums comprise the largest privately supported museum group on Long Island. They include three major exhibition buildings and a number of eighteenth- and nineteenth-century historic structures. Their overall theme is the exhibition and interpretation of American art and history. Thus, in the History Museum (H) there are special exhibitions on historical themes, a gallery of period rooms (in miniature), and a superb collection of antique decoys. The Art Museum (A) also features changing shows, along with permanent displays of works by William Sidney Mount (1807–1868), the celebrated Long Island genre painter.

The original heart of the complex is now known as the Carriage House (C). It displays over eighty vehicles illustrating the history of horse-drawn transportation. The carts, cabs, coaches, broughams, phaetons, wagons, sleighs, and fire engines are all a delight to see. The new Pleasure Driving Gallery helps make this one of the finest such collections in the country.

STONY BROOK

SMITHTOWN BAY

WEST MEADOW CREEK

West Meadow

Christian Avenue

PORPOISE CHANNEL

MUSEUMS

25A

North Country Road

Village

Main Street

Museums

Gristmill

25A

0   ¼   ½

Miles

When you visit Stony Brook (take Route 25A north from Smithtown), you can park either at the museum or on the waterfront. If you choose the former, go first to the History Museum (H) for admission tickets ($4.00 for adults). After seeing the three main buildings, you can also visit the blacksmith shop and schoolhouse and then take a short nature walk. Be sure to leave enough time to walk north along Main Street about a half mile into the village, passing the millpond with its resident families of waterfowl and water lilies, and stopping at the interesting old gristmill, which was recently restored to full operation. It is open from April through December; phone the Community Fund, which owns it, at 751–2244 for exact days and hours.

As you come to the village green you'll find a variety of interesting shops up on the right, and the waterfront ahead on the left. The bay and salt meadows here supply as New England a scene as you might imagine. It is not difficult to see how the English settlers who came here from Suffolk chose these shores or why it reminded them of their native country. It's also easy to understand the overwhelmingly important part played by the sea, bays, and water routes in the first two hundred years of Long Island's development.

Stony Brook village is clean and tidy and has an air of nostalgia. You can walk along, window-shopping and dating old houses as you head to your starting point, but surely you will have lost track of time on the way.

Although the museums are open all year, both hours and admission fees are subject to change. We suggest that you telephone in advance (751–0066) to get current information on hours and special exhibitions.

15

Sag Harbor

Sag Harbor, a National Historic District, is certainly one of the best-preserved old villages on Long Island, with hedges and picket fences and curving, crooked, and shaded streets that are lined with charming houses.

Starting at the Chamber of Commerce windmill on the waterfront, walk along Bay Street and on to the Long Wharf, observe the coastal activity, inspect the waterfront, shop at any one of the numerous little stores and markets in the area, or stroll in the Marine Park or yacht club area. If you wish, look across the harbor from the North Haven Bridge to Shelter Island in the north. Then walk up Main Street as far as you like. The finest example of Greek Revival architecture in New York State, built in 1845, now houses the revitalized Whaling and Historical Museum, which attracts more than 35,000 people seasonally. Across Garden Street is the Hannibal French House, a large Victorian mansion, now painted a pleasant, dark ivory color, and the old Custom House, now a National Landmark, the home and office of the first customs collector of New York State. Sag Harbor was named an official Port of Entry in 1789 by President George Washington, and a U.S. Post Office was initiated by Postmaster General Benjamin Franklin.

On side streets—wander off on any of them—you'll see many fine little houses built during prosperous days, late eighteenth to mid-nineteenth century. They have simple lines and the style of that era. These residential streets today, since many of the houses have been restored with care, painted, and nicely planted by their present owners, give you the feeling of the prosperity of the past.

You should turn left at the museum and go along Union Street past Madison to see the First Presbyterian Church of Sag Harbor, locally known as the Whalers Church, based on Egyptian style and something of a curiosity. The spyglass-shaped steeple that once dominated the town was blown down in the hurricane of 1938 and never replaced. All the architectural trim is said to be hand-carved by whalers from the village. And nearby, the old graveyard is interesting. A lovelier-looking church is Christ Episcopal farther down Madison.

First there was a little fishing village started here in 1665 by a small band of Narragansetts, traditional rivals of the Montauks and Shinnecocks. Then the white settlers moved in around 1707. Although known for a time as Sterling Bay (after the English Lord Sterling), it eventually took the name Sag Harbor, being the harbor of Sagg, a little settlement near what is now Bridgehampton, a contraction of the native name Saggabonac: "Where the Ground Nuts (Potatoes) Grow!"

At the end of the eighteenth century, Sag Harbor cleared a greater tonnage of goods than New York Harbor, and it was to become one of the principal whaling ports on the Atlantic seacoast, second only to New Bedford. Between 1790 and 1870 more than 500 voyages were made from here, and the whale oil brought back to light the cities and houses of New England was valued at $25 million. There were once sixty-three vessels registered here. The population reached 3,500 by 1843. Rough seamen walked these very streets you roam today—Montauk and Shinnecock Indians, but also Fiji Islanders, Hawaiians, Malays, Ethiopians, and Portuguese.

After the Civil War the whaling industry had a rapid decline, and Sag Harbor's fortunes dwindled. Today, tourism and light manufacturing are a boon.

16

Orient

Places on earth, like people, seem to develop under current conditions along conforming lines. One airport looks pretty much like any other, anywhere in our world, and cities and houses fall into similar categories. Those exceptions that guard their character from external forces, which have tendencies to change it, and preserve their antiquities develop an aura that is often admirable. Little villages lying somewhere along headwaters tend to preserve this aura, and the hamlet of Orient, lying the farthest east of any of the settlements on the northern fork, quite off the beaten track, has perhaps the greatest individuality of any place on Long Island. We hope, in saying this, that anyone will cautiously consider the trust we place in he who reads this. Don't rush right out to look. A swarm of people would be out of place in Orient. It also is a simple place; you won't be overwhelmed! The houses aren't as grand as those in Southampton or East Hampton. Property plots are rather small, and the antiques are not on a scale that would attract Sotheby's. It is not quaint, and there are no shops of any kind, other than a small general store and post office, closed Sundays. So you might be disappointed. But for us, Orient has a special character all its own.

If you go, you will leave Greenport on Route 25. The town of East Marion is 2 or 3 miles, and 3 miles beyond that, just after you cross the narrow causeway with Long Island Sound on your

left and Orient Harbor on your right, is the road (Village Lane) that leads down into the village. As you come to this causeway, you should stop at the parking place along the harbor, get out, and look. The map lays out well before you here. The village, from the distance, seems like one you'd see in Vermont. There are snowy white egrets that nest in the salt meadows and a peacefulness laid down on all the scene. We have read that Orient until after World War I was a favorite spot for honeymooners. Today it is primarily a quiet resort town.

Don't try to drive into town. Park off the road near the war memorial obelisk and the white church with the graceful steeple at the head of the lane. Then walk along the sidewalk. Houses, gardens, trees, and reflections will catch your eye. Orient has more than one hundred buildings built more than a century ago. Down the quiet, narrow, meandering Village Lane is the six-building museum complex that is run by the Oyster Ponds Historical Society (323–2480). The first building is the Village House Museum, a simple clapboard structure with a long widow's walk. It has early American furnishings and local collections and is clearly worth a visit. Behind it is the Hallock House with marine art, artifacts, and tools. Next door on a lawn is the Old Schoolhouse; across the street, the Webb House. Then there is the Red Barn, and so on.

The museum buildings are open from the end of June through September from 2:00 P.M. to 5:00 P.M. on Saturday and Sunday, and also on Wednesday and Thursday in July and August. Admission is $3.00.

After visiting the museum group, continue down the lane by the yacht club, and you can lengthen the walk as we do by continuing on out into the country fields and swinging back by a loop into the village.

Woodlands, Parks, and Preserves

The idea of finding a pleasant trail winding through quiet woods or open fields may seem hard to accept on this island of 2.6 million people in Nassau and Suffolk counties, yet the reality is that there are miles and miles of such walks to be enjoyed. Only a few are listed in this section, forming a starting point for further exploration. They are mostly in fairly large areas that have been saved from being paved with roads and houses by state or county acquisition and/or by The Nature Conservancy. The woods, roads, and trails are used by walkers, horseback riders, cyclists, birders, and joggers as an escape from urban pressures, and they serve this purpose well. Other sections in this volume list similar walks; the ones here are primarily those where water is not a prominent part of the scene.

Many of these areas have extensive trail networks that offer a great deal of variety in the details you can observe as well as in the flora and fauna. Others have nature trails, usually self-guiding, that can provide more of interest in a short distance than would be expected from simply wandering down an old road through a scrub oak woodland. In still others you'll find a long-distance trail passing through that, while interesting, doesn't lend itself to a loop walk that carries you back to the starting point over new terrain. As a consequence, while we've highlighted the walks that seem best for first acquaintance, do try others that show on our maps or on the maps that are often available at the park or preserve. We think you'll enjoy the variety, especially if you visit in different seasons of the year.

17

Garvies Point
Preserve and Museum

This sixty-two-acre area of glacial moraine has about 5 miles of marked nature trails over "the Carpenter Tract," purchased in 1668 from the Matinecock Indians. For thousands of years before this, woodland natives had hunted, gathered, and camped on this and adjoining lands. The concentrated remains of their middens here are one of the reasons Nassau County acquired the land in 1963 and opened the museum, which specializes in Native American archaeology as well as regional geology. Physically Garvies Point is similar in many ways to the Sands Point Preserve on the opposite side of Hempstead Harbor. It acquired the name from a former owner, Dr. Thomas Garvie, who emigrated from Scotland to Glen Cove in the early nineteenth century. The preserve is open daily 8:30 A.M. to dusk, but the museum is only open from 10:00 A.M. to 4:00 P.M. Wednesday through Saturday, and 1:00 to 4:00 P.M. on Sunday. Admission to the museum is $1.00 for adults and 50 cents for children.

A parking area adjoins the museum. Exhibits give you a fine introduction to Long Island before its discovery by Europeans. There is a sweeping view of Hempstead Harbor as you stand here at the museum, and the nature trails that start here provide good walking any time of year.

Although in the midst of suburban neighborhoods, the high ridge along the shore may set your mind to wondering about the state of the native people who stalked along it so many years ago. Those who greeted the settlers on Long Island were generally a congenial and helpful people and at first offered no resistance to the newcomers. Fish and game were plentiful, and they were adept at catching all that was needed. The northern climate here was ameliorated by the sea. Those early settlers recognized the advantages and were joined rather quickly by others who learned about the place. The history of these early days is well documented, and your local library may start you reading about these first encounters between the European settlers and the Native Americans.

During the warmer months, the preserve is full of wildlife; the woods and meadows attract a great variety of birds. Because there's an effort to keep it in a natural state, a wide variety of native plants grow here. You'll find forty-eight species of trees, including northern red oak, pin oak, sassafras, beech, black cherry, persimmon, tulip tree, locust, sycamore, butternut hickory. It is all in all a very pleasant experience to roam over these unexpected riches.

If you walk along the seashore, you can inspect the rocky beach and the bluffs above it. It contains the glacial debris so characteristic of all the North Shore. Only a few spots on Long Island, however, have glacial deposits so unusually thin as they are here at Garvies Point, thus exposing 70-million-year-old deposits of sand, silts, and multicolored clays. Well-preserved fossils of Cretaceous plants have even been found along these shorefront cliffs.

From Long Island Expressway, Northern State Parkway, Northern Boulevard, or Meadowbrook Parkway, exit on Glen Cove Road, northbound. Continue on Glen Cove bypass (Route 107 north, keep left at fork) to last traffic light facing Glen Cove Fire House. Turn right and follow signs to the museum (671–0300).

18

Muttontown Preserve

Under the stewardship of the Nassau County Museum, this 550-acre preserve combines the assets of a number of old North Shore estates to provide a quiet, rural, and startlingly extensive area for woodland walks. Situated in East Norwich south of Route 25A and west of Route 106, it comprises four principal areas, two of which are of primary interest to walkers.

The first of these is the fifty-acre Nature Center area, which features a marked self-guiding trail running through an irregular U-shaped parcel that largely surrounds one of the old mansions, Chelsea, which is now used for selected cultural exhibitions and affairs. The Nature Center proper (571–8500) is at the end of Muttontown Lane, a little road running south off 25A in East Norwich. There's parking space for the center and for walkers in the preserve; the gate is open 9:30 A.M. to 4:30 P.M. daily. Behind the center is a little pond that was dug in 1967 to provide better drainage to the wet area here, and deciduous woods of swamp maple, pin oak, and tupelo, the tree closely related to the sourgum of southern swamps that turns scarlet in autumn. Although the pond doesn't support any fish, it does provide the environment needed by a variety of beetles and other insects and attracts turtles, frogs, and salamanders, as well as a variety of birds.

Happily the trails are marked with colored number posts, and this is most helpful to guide you along twisty, turny paths where otherwise you might miss seeing much the area offers.

North Hempstead Turnpike

25A

MUTTONTOWN PRESERVE

Muttontown Lane

Parking

Nature Center

106

N

Walled Garden

½

¼

Parking

Ruins

106

0

Miles

Muttontown Road

Many of the trees are marked, too, for identification. Watch out for poison ivy, which grows rankly throughout the preserve!

Follow the green markers for trail 1 through the swamp area where you will find arrowwood and spicebush growing, along with ferns, mosses, and liverworts, and you will come out on a large field, once farmland, now let go so that it attracts bobwhite and pheasant, field mice and red fox, and turn right here following the green blazes into the evergreen woods. On the hot summer day we walked here the cool of this woods was noticeable. It is a forest of white pine and larch, with a scattering of dogwood and black cherry, and paths are spongy, good walking, so you stride forth with an easy gait.

Don't be upset if you lose your sense of direction. The path actually doubles back, and you find yourself turned around heading north on the green trail, which goes nearly back to Route 25A, before returning. Part way along you can cross over on the yellow marker (#4) if you prefer a shorter walk.

The other major area for walking is the contiguous 200-acre parcel south of the Nature Center trails down to Muttontown Road. The trails in this area are mainly bridle paths left over from the days when all this was horsey country. They are mostly marked with colored and numbered posts as they wind through evergreen woods and open meadows, past glacially formed rolling hills and kettle-hole ponds. This section has its own parking area, entered from Route 106 about 1,000 feet north of the Muttontown Road intersection. This large lot is still actively used for horse trailers and supports both hikers and users of the equestrian practice areas.

This part of the preserve, along with 250 acres south of Muttontown Road that are not open for general use, comprised the Lansdell Christie estate. Some overgrown ruins in the woods north of Muttontown Road are the only remaining evidence of a mansion there that was once owned (but never used) by King Zog of Albania.

If everyone who walks here comes as a guest and is concerned and aware of the life preserved here, we shall have a treasured little sanctuary forever wild.

19

Uplands Farm Sanctuary

The Long Island Chapter of The Nature Conservancy (367–3225) has its headquarters in farm buildings that are surrounded by open fields and upland woods on Lawrence Hill Road, in Cold Spring Harbor, about ¼ mile east of the junction of Routes 25A and 108. There are trails through the preserve that not only visit varied terrain, but also connect with the Nassau-Suffolk Greenbelt Trail to permit a 1½-mile loop walk. A detailed guide is available. The office is open weekdays 9:00 A.M. to 5:00 P.M., but the trails are open daily dawn to dusk.

We wrote briefly about The Nature Conservancy in the preface to this edition. Though it is a national organization, it works quietly and most effectively on the local level, and the two chapters on Long Island have been responsible for the acquisition of more than seventy natural areas here, many of them ecologically fragile. The Sunken Forest on Fire Island, the North Shore Wildlife Sanctuary, and a section of Caumsett State Park are all properties that The Nature Conservancy helped to set aside for conservation purposes.

We have walked a number of these natural areas that belong to the Conservancy with great satisfaction, and they are open to serious walkers with permits. If interested, you should contact them directly. With your help as a member even more can be accomplished.

TARGET ROCK NATIONAL
WILDLIFE REFUGE

Target Rock

HUNTINGTON BAY

Marsh

LLOYD HARBOR

Target Rock Road

Hawk Drive

Forrest Drive

Lloyd Harbor Road

Miles

0   ¼   ½

20

Target Rock
National Wildlife Refuge

This interesting refuge is, like Morton National Wildlife Refuge, managed by the U.S. Fish and Wildlife Service to preserve endangered plants and animals, to preserve natural diversity, and to perpetuate migratory bird life. It covers eighty heavily wooded and rolling acres at the eastern end of Lloyd Neck and contains about .3 mile of beach on Huntington Bay south of Fort Point and Target Rock.

The refuge was once the estate of financier Ferdinand Eberstadt, who built a thirty-five-room neo-Georgian mansion there in 1937 on one of the higher points. After his death the property was deeded to the government in 1967 as a wildlife refuge. There is a ½-mile trail to the beach that goes through mature oak-hickory woods and passes close to a brackish pond that always has a few waterfowl in residence. There is also a ¼-mile side trail around the knob where the old mansion once sat. Along the trail is a grove of magnificent tall oaks.

The refuge is very popular with wildlife. All told, naturalists have identified over 300 species of birds, mammals, reptiles, and amphibians in the area.

The main trails are broad and easy to manage even as you stay on the lookout for wildlife; if you stay clear of grass at the beach, your risk of acquiring a tick should be minimal. There used to be a number of other woodland trails, including one that ran along the bluff overlooking the bay, but heavy use disturbed the wild creatures, and so the trails have reluctantly been closed to the public.

When you look north along the beach, you'll see two large boulders just offshore. They were once part of the glacial residue in the morainal bluff above them, but the land has eroded to the west to leave them in the bay. At the time of the American Revolution the bigger one was still up in the bank, but exposed, so British warships offshore used it as a gunnery target—hence the name Target Rock.

The refuge is open daily from 8:00 A.M. to dusk. It can be reached by following West Neck Road and Lloyd Harbor Road 2.2 miles past the entrance to Caumsett State Park. Questions? Call 271–2409, or if no answer, call 286–0485 at the National Wildlife Refuge headquarters. There is no entrance fee at this writing, but $4.00 per car may be charged in the future.

21

Caleb Smith
State Park Preserve

This 543-acre tract dates back to 1663, when the first Smith bought the land from the Indians. Smith ownership continued for over 200 years until Caleb started selling parts of it to the Brooklyn Gun Club (later the Wyandanch Club). By 1900 the club had all the land and had completed their expansion of the original house to what you now see as the museum building. The property was bought by New York State in 1963 as part of a planned program of open space preservation. It is now open for "passive" recreation as an environmental preserve with ponds, a number of trails (including the Long Island Greenbelt and two self-guiding nature trails), and a modest museum in the main building.

A permit is required and can be obtained at the museum (in the imposing old clubhouse) when you pay the $1.00 per person entrance fee. Park hours are 8:00 A.M. to 4:30 P.M.; it's open Wednesday through Sunday all year, and also on Tuesday, April through September. The phone number is 265–1054. In case you plan to walk through the part of the preserve that is south of Route 25, be sure when you get your permit to get the combination for the locked gates you will encounter when you enter or leave that part.

CALEB SMITH
STATE PARK
PRESERVE

Meadow Road

PHILLIPS MILL
POND

W

25

Museum

NISSEQUOGUE RIVER

W

W

WILLOW
POND

Blydenburgh State Park

W

W

W

N

0   1/10   2/10   3/10

Miles

The preserve is bisected by Jericho Turnpike (Route 25), which runs in a curve southwesterly here. The entrance, which is not prominent, is off the northern side of the highway 3 miles east of the Sagtikos State Parkway. Drive slowly and keep a sharp lookout for the entrance after you pass Old Willets Path.

One other survivor from colonial times (not open to the public) is the Aron Vail House, which was an inn on the old stagecoach route and a point of interest in early Smithtown history. On both sides of Route 25 the preserve is made up of swamp and upland and provides a fine habitat for many geese and ducks, a wide variety of birds, rabbits, raccoons, and native wildlife. We found the undulating trail soft and pleasant footing, remarkably quiet in one of the busiest sections of Suffolk County.

On our walk here we followed a number of trails blazed for cross-country skiing and stayed mostly on the northwest side of the preserve. These rolling slopes and hillsides are the northern side of the Ronkonkoma Moraine, and the drainage flows into the Nissequogue River, and into the Long Island Sound.

The part of the preserve south of Route 25A, where the Nissequogue meanders through ponds and lowlands, was a mecca for fly fishermen when it was a private club. It is now open to the public on a strict reservation basis and still provides excellent fishing.

CONNETQUOT RIVER
STATE PARK PRESERVE

N

L.I.R.R.

Veterans Memorial Highway

454

W

0   ½   1

Miles

CONNETQUOT RIVER

W

Bunces Bridge

W

Hatchery

W

MAIN
POND

SLADE
POND

Pond Road

Sunrise
Highway

27

Montauk
Highway

27A

22

Connetquot River
State Park Preserve

Connetquot River State Park Preserve is an ideal place to walk. It has a very special place in the Long Island State Park system; the designated term "preserve" means that there are no ball fields or playgrounds or picnic areas. The idea is to keep an area like this much as it has always been and to limit its use to "passive recreation," such as walking, horseback riding, fishing. Bicycles are not permitted here.

In order to keep the character of the preserve undisturbed, walkers are required to get a permit in advance. Write to Connetquot River State Park, P.O. Box 505, Oakdale, NY 11769, giving name, address, and number of people in the party. The permit (good for a year) can be picked up at the gate when you arrive and pay the daily admission fee of $1.00 per adult. The park is open year-round Wednesday through Sunday 8:00 A.M. to 4:30 P.M., and from April 1 through Labor Day it is also open Tuesday. If you have questions, call 581–1005.

A word about getting to its obscure entrance off the Sunrise Highway, Route 27, which is a double two-lane highway, each headed in opposite directions: You must be in the westbound lanes, so if you are headed east, reverse direction at Pond Road east of the entrance (at a traffic light), and look sharp for the white pavement markings of a very short exit lane.

An explanation of how an oasis this size, nearly 3,500 acres, is possible is in the deed, which was held by a syndicate of wealthy sportsmen as a private trout stream and hunting preserve for well over one hundred years. Before that, it was held as a patent dating back to pre-Revolutionary times. When you leave your car at the parking lot and stroll out by the buildings near the entrance booth, you will be seeing what was the clubhouse and what has been available to public access only since 1978. In days gone by, others who have walked these trails whom you just might have heard of include Daniel Webster, Ulysses S. Grant, General Sherman, Lorenzo Delmonico, and Charles L. Tiffany, to name a few—membership was limited to one hundred names at any time.

We headed out on the red blazed trail—there are miles and miles of trails including a section of the north-to-south Long Island Greenbelt Trail—catching glimpses of the Connetquot River as we went along. It was late November, and all the migrating birds had passed through, but we saw hooded merganser, mallard, swan, and a female wood duck. We saw three deer, surprised two rabbits, a squirrel, and a fox.

"It was a red fox. We have them here," Gil Bergen, the park superintendent who has managed the place for many years, told us. "You are lucky to see one in the daytime."

On a recent spring visit our day was made complete by a close encounter with a couple of wild turkeys, the tom in gorgeous multicolor display—and the hen trudging slowly along behind. It was an uncommon and beautiful sight.

23

Three Parks with Views

To suggest climbing hills on Long Island may appear frivolous, but since we have an urge to reach heights and see the view from there, it occurs to us that others may, too. That's why we're suggesting these three morainal hills that command unusual views for this area. West Hills County Park boasts Jayne's Hill, at 401.5 feet above sea level, the highest point on Long Island. Next comes Colonie Hill in Islip's Hidden Pond Park (180 feet), and then Bald Hill (285 feet) in Suffolk Hills Country Park.

Jayne's Hill is in the northeast corner of West Hills Park, a heavily wooded area with an extensive network of blazed trails and wood roads that justify visiting it even without a view. The view is limited in width, but it is a fine outlook to the southwest, with the Atlantic, 13 miles away, easily seen on a clear day.

It's possible to drive nearly to the top of Jayne's Hill by finding Walt Whitman's old house off Route 110 in Melville (look for historic markers), and then going directly west from there (after a visit!) on West Hills Road, and in three blocks turning left on Reservoir Road. This road rises steeply to end just below the top. Follow a footpath on the left side of the water tank to the high point.

If you'd like more exercise than this, then go to the park office for a free copy of a detailed trail map. The office is on High Hold Drive; get there from Jericho Turnpike (Route 25) by going south on Round Swamp Road 0.4 miles and turning left onto High Hold, or else try back roads west from Route 110. If you

then wish to explore the park or just hike up to Jayne's Hill, follow the map to reach Sweet Hollow Road and then go south on it to a parking and picnic area just beyond a big riding stable. By a variety of trails Jayne's Hill is a bit more than a mile away.

The second lookout is Colonie Hill in Hauppage where the Long Island Greenbelt Trail crossed the Ronkonkoma Moraine and passes through Hidden Pond Park. Here there are woodlands closely surrounded by "civilization," but the pleasant view north is won by a very short walk (under .25 mile) from where the trail crosses Motor Parkway. To get there go east on Motor Parkway from exit 37 of the Long Island Expressway, (Route 495) to a point 1.2 miles beyond the intersection with Route 454. When you see some major high-tension lines crossing overhead, stop and park. There is an opening in the fence there where the white-blazed Greenbelt heads north. Follow it; when the trail turns west along the ridge line, you'll find the views, and a couple of benches to help you enjoy them. The body of the park is down below on the north side of the moraine; parking is available there too.

The final lookout, Bald Hill, is about 3.5 miles south of Riverhead just off Route 51. It's in an undeveloped county park, but close to the highway, so it's easy to find. You have two choices here on ways to the top. If you want a quick and easy trip (climb 130 feet in 0.2 mile) park your car off the road by the gates 0.6 miles south of the Routes 51 and 88 split. Go in past the barriers and follow the heavily worn road directly away from the highway. After about 600 feet there is a broad trail (jeep road) on your left heading nearly straight uphill. Take it, and in just a few minutes you'll be on top with a fine view northeast through a gap in the pines. Peconic Bay, Robins Island, and Shelter Island will all be visible on a good day. This whole venture should take about half an hour.

If instead you'd like to get an invigorating 2-mile walk in addition to the climb, go left on Route 88 when you reach it from Riverhead. After 0.3 mile turn in at the entrance to Suffolk Community College and go right into the big east parking field and head for the northwest corner, where there is a fine, roofed map and notice board. Park there and follow a clear but poorly maintained yellow-blazed nature trail roughly north to and along the west edge of a big glacial kettle hole. At a junction with the white-blazed Pine Barrens Trail (Paumanok Path), go left on it, cross Route 51, and follow the trail southwest, parallel to Route 51, until you come to an area of heavily torn-up wood roads. There you will easily find the short way up the northeast face of Bald Hill. An alternative route from that area is to follow other trails around the right (west) face of the knob until you find one that goes basically due east as it makes a more gradual climb to the top. This route means a 3-mile round-trip from your car, with a fair amount of up and down as well.

You'll find many roads leading off into these woods. Extend your walks and enjoy them while you can, but don't get lost—it's easy to do in the Pine Barrens. In fact, if you're serious about exploring this area, we suggest you contact the Long Island Greenbelt Trail Conference (see p. x) to get a copy of their Long Island Pine Barrens Trail map or any other current offerings. U.S. Geological Survey maps are good too, but are not nearly as complete or up-to-date with trail information,

24

Sears-Bellows County Park

Sears-Bellows lies to the north of the Sunrise Highway (Route 27) and south of the Flanders Road (Route 24), but fortunately has enough acreage to offer a feeling of remoteness, complete with two lakes, some ponds, and lots of cover for deer and game birds, including the marvelously colored wood duck. Walking here is most pleasant in spring or fall, but people are essentially gregarious, we have observed, and like to be where the crowd is, enjoying the fishing and boating at the big lake, Bellows. Thus, even when we walk here in season, in a few easy strides away from the camping area you lose almost everyone.

You will find parking spaces here, as in all Suffolk County parks, limited in season to Suffolk Country residents with permits. Trails are not heavy traffic areas, and hikers are not discouraged, so if you do not have the permit, the rangers will usually treat you courteously if you yourselves are not a nuisance.

The park is open daily all year, but it may have shorter daily hours off-season. Check with the park office at 852–8290 if you're concerned.

The best entry to the park is on Bellows Pond Road off the Flanders Road (Route 24), 5 miles south of the Riverhead traffic circle and 1.8 miles from exit 65 on Route 27.

Many service roads make good paths through the woodlands and around the lakes, and if it is a quiet day when you come,

Spinny Road

W

SEARS POND

MILL CREEK

24

W

HOUSE
POND

BELLOWS POND

GRASS
POND

Riverhead-Hampton Bays

Road

HUBBARD CREEK

PENNY
POND

W

Sunrise Highway

Bellows Pond Road

27

SEARS BELLOWS
COUNTY PARK

To 80

½

¼

Miles

0

the walk around Bellows Pond is an easy one. Our favorite walk, however, is from Bellows to Sears Pond, following the white-blazed Pine Barrens Trail, and lingering before returning. The paths are especially nice for walking, pine needles underfoot, wide, and unobstructed. Go north first through woods, where we always seem to flush out a grouse or two, past a pond on the right that is a favorite haunt of the wood duck, then swing to the left and into a clearing that has a significant rise of land on it. We usually climb the rise and sit for a few minutes because there often seems to be a red-tailed hawk here circling, and there is a view of the surrounding country. We rejoin the path on the other side of the hill and walk about a mile northwestward through sparse, burned-over woods. The growth and vegetation increases heavily as you come to Sears Pond. Go down to the water quietly; the ducks are wary in this secluded hideaway. If you have the patience to sit in the duck blinds, there are always interesting comings and goings on the water.

Although it is quiet enough to listen to the birdsong and hear the flapping of the duck's wing, the muffled traffic noises from the two highways do carry across the treetops, as do jet sounds of overhead planes on their route to New York and punctuations from monstrous earth-moving equipment or chain saws. This is true, of course, anyplace on Long Island, and Sears-Bellows is as free today of the sounds of our civilization as almost anywhere else. So we can be grateful for the relative calm and tranquility and hope that others, too, will recognize it and strive to perpetuate it. And be thankful for the settings provided for public use by a foresighted County Park Commission.

MASHOMACK PRESERVE

COECLES HARBOR

CEDAR ISLAND COVE

N

Route 114

Visitor Center

SMITH COVE

SHELTER ISLAND SOUND

Nicholl Point

GARDINERS BAY

Lodge

Ferry

Route 114

MAJOR'S HARBOR

To SAG HARBOR

LONG ISLAND SOUND

Shelter Island

Mashomack Point

0   ¼   ½   ¾   1

Miles

Mashomack Preserve

Mashomack is unique. In its 2,000 acres of woodlands, marshes, and tidal creeks it provides a greater variety of habitats and a greater variety of birds than any other area in Long Island. It occupies the southeastern third of Shelter Island, between the twin forks, and so can only be reached by a short ferry ride (South Ferry is closer and quicker than North Ferry). We are able to enjoy it only because it was purchased in 1980 by the Nature Conservancy from a far-seeing family.

The feature most notable, other than the tremendous scenic beauty of the preserve, is its vastness. Walking on some of the 17 miles of trails here, it's hard to believe you are only 90 miles from New York City. At Mashomack, together with protected areas to the south around Northwest Harbor, a maritime environment of unsurpassed richness has been given a fighting chance. The area's extensive salt marshes are vitally significant as a breeding ground and nursery for organisms at the bottom of the food chain, upon which all other life depends.

Four well-marked trails offer hikes of varying lengths and difficulty, up to 11 miles. All of them start at the Visitor Center, in the entrance area. On weekends volunteer naturalists can answer questions about natural history and the archaeology of the preserve. The gift shop is soon to be joined by a museum and teaching center overlooking a kettle hole. There will also be a trail for the handicapped and visually impaired, featuring a wide variety of native plants.

Mashomack can easily be reached from either north or south as Route 114 connects both ferries. The preserve entrance is on the east side of the road, 0.9 mile from the South Ferry. The Visitor Center is but a short walk from the parking area. It and the preserve are open daily, from dawn to dusk, from May to September, and on weekends year-round, with a suggested donation of $1.50 for adults. For further information call 749–1001.

The majority of the preserve is upland oak and beech forest, which includes a rare pine swamp complex, the only community of its kind known to occur on Long Island. There is almost no open water in this wetland, and all of the plants are rooted in a floating mat of sphagnum moss. Because of its ability to retain many times its own weight in water, sphagnum moss plays an important part in keeping wetlands moist during dry periods. The swamp is fringed by water willows growing in muck surrounding a diverse shrub layer, where swamp azalea, highbush blueberry, white alder, winterberry, and mountain holly, unusual for Long Island, can be found.

An abundance of bird life makes Mashomack a paradise for ornithologists. As many as eighty-two breeding species have been recorded, and fifty-six different species winter at the preserve. To truly appreciate Mashomack, it is important to visit during all of the seasons and at different times of the day. Spring is marked by the return of the first pairs of ospreys from South America. More than any other creature, they represent the wild spirit of Mashomack. They can be seen all along the shores plunging down for fish and circling triumphantly with their catch. Summer is when most visitors come, and an early morning walk will be filled with birdsong in the upland areas.

In the autumn, hundreds of black ducks, Canada geese, and other migrating birds stop over at Mashomack. This is one of the best times for bird-watching, as the fall foliage provides a backdrop of exploding colors; the scarlet of red maple and sweet gum, golden beech leaves, red dogwoods, and orange bittersweet.

Winter offers an excellent opportunity for tracking deer, fox, raccoon, and even mink, which leave their signatures in the snow. The more adventurous can follow the trail along Gardiners Bay and catch a glimpse of harbor seals basking on rocks in the winter sun.

HITHER HILLS STATE PARK

NAPEAGUE BAY

Railroad

FRESH POND

WALKING DUNES

Goff Point

NAPEAGUE HARBOR

Overlook

Old Montauk/ Highway

ATLANTIC OCEAN

Montauk Highway

27

Miles

0   ¼   ½   ¾   1

26

Hither Hills State Park

The Hither Hills area that we deal with here contains a 1,755-acre state park and two preserves totaling 1,340 acres. They come at the east end of the long, narrow finger of land that connects the prehistoric Montauk Island with the South Fork at Amagansett. The state park includes the long, sandy triangle that is the eastern shore of Napeague Harbor, the western half of the morainal upland, and about 1.3 miles of ocean and campground to the south. The balance of the upland, extending a bit over two miles along the north side of Montauk Parkway (Route 27), contains two contiguous preserves under the jurisdiction of The Nature Conservancy. The whole area has many sand roads and trails in the mixed pine-oak forest and natural features and wildlife that make it attractive to the walker. There is too much to see in one day, so you should plan ahead and come armed with maps and data that will make your visit more rewarding.

When you first arrive here, make a point of stopping for a few minutes at the overlook on Route 27, on your left as you reach the highest level of the moraine (the second crest). Leave your car to survey the panorama and get oriented. In the foreground you'll find a grassy area with a few trees that was decimated in a 1986 forest fire, and is now recovered but not a forest yet. Beyond it you have a good view of Napeague Harbor, with the Atlantic on the left, and the southwest end of Block Island Sound and Gardiners Island to the right. This is also a good central place to park while you explore the park and preserves (no parking along Route 27, technically a parkway).

The western triangle has the harbor shore on the west, a long beach facing Block Island Sound on the north, and wooded uplands on the east. There are two areas to visit here that you will enjoy. The first is the Walking Dunes, an interesting group of sand hills that are very gradually creeping across the flat terrain in response to prevailing northwest winds. As they move they gradually cover the trees in their path, while the trees respond by growing taller. It's probably a draw most of the time. The advancing face of the dunes is beautifully rounded and smooth, while there's a nice view from the dune crest. To find the dunes, look for a lone railroad grade crossing with gates at the east end of the long, straight stretch on Route 27 from Amagansett, just before the hills begin. Take the paved road over the crossing and proceed straight north to the end of the pavement, about .75 mile. Park on the side of the road there and take the trail that heads east from that point. You'll be at the side of a steep dune in only a few hundred feet. Ill-defined paths through the trees and underbrush to the right will enable you to climb up the side without too much fuss, but do avoid disturbing the advancing face of the dunes by walking there.

The route to Goff Point is obvious along the harbor shore, but for an easier path, follow the shore for only a few hundred yards beyond the pavement until there's a gap in the sand bank on the right. Go through the gap and you will soon find a firm interior sand road that makes for easy walking either to the point or to the northern shore.

Another nice place to visit is Fresh Pond, a favorite with fishermen, birds, and other animals. Probably the beast route to the pond is by the trails and roads from the overlook. Use the East Hampton Trails map (see p. 91 for more information) as your guide, and you should have little trouble.

The two preserves that lie to the east of the state park begin where the power line heads northeast and downhill from Route

27 a short distance east of the overlook. They offer several miles of woods roads, easy trails, and bayside bluffs. To visit these preserves the best place to park is at the entrance to the town recycling center, 2 miles east of the overlook on Route 27. Park just off the highway close to, but not in front of, the barred road on the left that leads to the interior.

Your enjoyment of the Hither Hills area will be greatly enhanced if, before you arrive there, you buy two very useful items. One is an excellent Hither Hills Trail Map that you can get from the town clerk at the East Hampton town offices, at 159 Pantigo Road (Route 27). It is the key to not getting misplaced in the woods! The other is the "South Fork–Shelter Island Preserve Guide" issued by the Nature Conservancy, P.O. Box 5125, East Hampton, NY 11937. It's an excellent 75-page booklet that tells you a great deal about 28 preserves in the South Fork areas east of Southampton. It has details on how to find each preserve, trail directions, and what is interesting about each from a naturalist's viewpoint.

Some practical information about the park and preserves is that they are open daily, without charge, all year. You should know, however, that hunting is permitted at various times in the park during the late fall and winter. We suggest you call the park office at 668–2461 or 668–5000 to find out the exact dates of the open seasons for various types of game. Another good source of information is the New York State Department of Environmental Conservation in Stony Brook (444–0273), which issues the necessary hiking permits.

Former Estates

In the era beginning about 1900 and extending through the twenties, literally hundreds of wealthy people bought tracts of land on Long Island to create estates for themselves. The favored areas were along the shores of the Sound and in the gentle hills of Nassau and western Suffolk, north of the main arteries such as Jericho Turnpike and the railroad. It is estimated that at least 500 major properties were acquired and mansions built on this Gold Coast, surely a unique suburban concentration.

Today, however, it is a different story. Population pressure and financial problems have resulted in most of the estates being broken up, mansions being demolished, and more modest homes being built (some still costing in the millions) in the spaces thus freed. A few of the big houses were acquired by schools, colleges, religious institutions, and various other public bodies. In some cases the land remains undisturbed but the mansion has vanished, as you will note from some of the walks in this section. In others, the mansion remains essentially unchanged and competes with the landscaped grounds for your attention.

This pattern of dividing and altering estates holds for all but one, Blydenburgh. It had remained, until 1938, under the ownership of a single family since Colonial times. As a result the house is not grand, but it has a fine setting overlooking the pond and mill that brought the owners their prosperity.

If you are intrigued by these estates, as we were, you might like to visit your library to read an elegant volume by Monica Randall entitled *Mansions of Long Island's Gold Coast*. It has descriptions and photographs of a generous cross-section of these estates, of their owners, and of their fates. It's a fascinating book.

27

U.S. Merchant
Marine Academy

Although fenced and entered through a guarded gate, the U.S. Merchant Marine in Kings Point is open to the public daily from 8:30 A.M. to 5:30 P.M., and the eighty-two-acre grounds, formerly the estate of automobile magnate Walter P. Chrysler, make for a pleasant visit. The young American men and women who have the good fortune to get their education at this beautiful place should count themselves lucky in many ways. They have a stunning 180-degree view of Long Island Sound—the daintily soaring spans of the Throgs Neck and Whitestone bridges and the cubes and rectangles of Manhattan. The campus includes docks with an impressive variety of boats used by officers-in-training to gain the experience necessary to handle any kind of vessel.

There are three buildings that deserve a visit, all on the bluff overlooking the sound and waterfront. To the south is the handsome Memorial Chapel, near it the white administrative center (Wiley Hall) which was Walter P. Chrysler's residence for many years, and at the north end the American Merchant Marine Museum. It features a history of the academy, an exceptionally fine collection of over fifty ship models, and other memorabilia. The curator is Frank Braynard, the noted marine author, artist, and lecturer. The museum (773–5515) is open Tuesday and Wednesday 11:00 A.M. to 3:00 P.M. and Saturday and Sunday 1:00 to 4:30 P.M., but it is closed from the middle of June to the middle of August and on federal holidays.

The academy is located on Steamboat Road, facing Long Island Sound, and a circuit of the campus makes an interesting, easy walk. If they appeal to you, you may watch regimental reviews some Saturday mornings in the spring and fall (773–5000).

As for the training here, it is 100 percent science and engineering. The graduate achieves a Bachelor of Science degree, a U.S. Coast Guard license as a Third Mate or a Third Assistant Engineer, and a commission as Ensign in the U.S. Naval Reserve. There is no tuition. The ages of the students range from seventeen to twenty-five. The daily routine begins at 6:10 A.M., with classes 8:00 to 12:00 and 1:30 to 5:00; lights off at 9:45. The school offers independent study and sea training on board merchant vessels. Two graduates who chose other careers after spending their early years at sea are J. Lane Kirkland '42, former president of the AFL-CIO, and Dr. Thomas Nicholson '42, who became director of the American Museum of Natural History.

28

Sands Point Preserve

Comprising 216 acres of prime Long Island real estate, Sands Point Preserve stands on splendid bluffs overlooking Long Island Sound at the mouth of Hempstead Harbor just north of Port Washington. For walkers it has six short blazed trails and a small pond on land that supports a surprisingly wide range of plants and bird life. There is a mile of beachfront to explore as well. It is said that geologists find much of interest along here, in case you have rock-hounding tendencies. In the wooded areas there are native trees that were here when the first settlers arrived and also specimen oriental varieties that were brought in at the turn of the century.

No doubt these acres were groomed and manicured when the Goulds and then the Guggenheims lived here, but they are wilder now. There are two old manor houses and a large structure built to resemble a castle, Ireland's Kilkenny Castle in fact, but to serve as a stable. Today this building houses a small museum and also serves as the repository of all manner of interesting items of furniture, carriages, and assorted pieces inherited by the Nassau County Department of Recreation and Parks and stored here. It is worth a ramble through.

The two mansions, one (Hempstead House) built by the Gould family, were subsequently owned by the Guggenheims. Harry Guggenheim, who was an early flying enthusiast and ad-

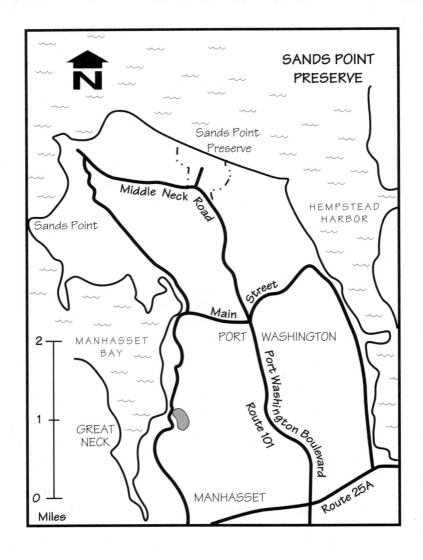

mirer of the young Charles A. Lindbergh, owned one. Harry's home (Falaise) was the scene of many gracious social gatherings, for he was an outgoing man with many influential friends. When Lindbergh completed his historic flight across the Atlantic and returned to America; he was hard pressed to find any escape from the mobs who awaited him everywhere he went. Harry Guggenheim gave him sanctuary at Falaise. The strong friendship that developed between these two, the worldly and sophisticated older man and the inexperienced, shy young flier, is a remarkable story, too long to tell here.

Since Sands Point is an easy commute to New York and yet presents the aura of gracious country living together with access to the water and fine water views, the private homes out here tend to be large, protectively landscaped, and very expensive. So it is indeed a privilege to have this fine old estate open to the public. Imagine 216 acres to wander about in where every inch of territory is so valuable.

Since Falaise can only be seen on an escorted tour, you'll need to plan ahead. It is a comfortable and cozy Norman French country house, well worth a visit, and it shows the owners' gracious lifestyle. Conducted hourly, tours require advance reservations and cost an extra $4.00 beyond the admission fee to the preserve. They're conducted in the afternoons; children under twelve are not permitted.

The preserve is managed by the Nassau County Department of Recreation and Parks. Because of financial belt-tightening, its museum is not normally open in the winter, though the grounds remain open without charge. In general, the museum season runs from May through October ($6.00 fee), with some special exhibits earlier or later. Daily hours are from 10:00 A.M. to 5:00 P.M.; closed Monday. For information on current events and for Falaise tour reservations (afternoons only), call 571–7900.

NASSAU COUNTY
MUSEUM OF ART

N

L.I.R.R.

25A

Entrance

Educational
Center

Parking

Pinetum

Museum Annex

Museum

Parking

Formal
Gardens

Miles

0   1/10   2/10

29

Nassau County Museum of Art

It wouldn't surprise us if William Cullen Bryant had been sitting on the very site of today's Nassau County Museum of Art when he wrote:

> *To him who, in the love of Nature, holds*
> *Communion with her visible forms, she speaks*
> *A various language.*

This was once his farmland, and he loved wandering over it. Today, nature's visible forms still show themselves in nice variety, and a walk here is a quieting experience, even though it lies just off the busy thoroughfare of Northern Boulevard.

The Nassau County Museum of Art now occupies an imposing Georgian mansion on the hilltop that was last owned by the son of Henry Clay Frick, a co-founder of U.S. Steel. He lived there for nearly fifty years and did much to improve the main building and the surrounding 145 acres of woodland and meadow. He had an active interest in nature, kept a variety of animals and birds, and planted a fine pinetum that still survives today. The property was bought by Nassau County after his death in 1965, and the main house was converted to its present use thereafter.

The museum is well worth visiting to see the changing special exhibitions, which are the primary attractions. Predominantly keyed to modern art, they offer interesting views into many facets of the art world. Recent exhibitions have included *La Belle Epoque* and *Treasures of Czar and Czarina*. It is good to phone before visiting, since the museum proper is usually closed for brief periods while a new exhibit is hung. The grounds, of course, are always open. The best introduction to them is by first walking the perimeter road (a 1-mile loop) to get the lay of the land. Then explore the open fields and informal paths through the woods. There are no marked trails, but you should visit the pinetum as well as the formal garden next to the parking lot. On the northwest side of the grounds you may spot a striking Gothic Revival cottage that Bryant had built in 1862 (now being restored).

One striking feature of the area is the presence of nearly thirty modern sculptures in natural settings throughout the grounds. Some were commisioned, others are on extended loan, but all provide an interesting contrast to the parklike background. You can get a "sculpture map" at the museum to guide you.

Do walk through the Pinetum. It is more than just a shady place to stroll. In its heyday under Mr. Frick, it had more than 190 species of conifers, making it one of the best collections in America. Today it is mature and less exceptional, but it is still interesting and instructive to walk down the central corridor to see the seven species group (firs, pines, hemlocks, spruces, cypresses, and cedars). A leaflet with more details should be available at the museum.

The museum entrance is clearly marked on Northern Boulevard (just east of the railroad overpass at the top of the rise from the Roslyn Village area), and there is ample free parking. It is open Tuesday through Sunday from 11:00 A.M. to 5:00 P.M., and admission is $2.00 for adults, less for seniors and students. There is a pleasant small cafe in one wing, though you might be tempted to bring a sandwich to enjoy on a hillside near the woods. Museum information? Call 484–9338.

30

Old Westbury Gardens

Long Island is fortunate in that of the 500 estates that were built on the north shore Gold Coast between 1900 and 1925, two of the very best remain for us to enjoy, Old Westbury Gardens and Planting Fields Arboretum. Both have gracious mansions, and both have superb landscapes and gardens that we can envy and perhaps copy (in parts). Both are large enough in area and diverse enough in their features to permit strolling about, endlessly finding new aspects to admire.

On balance, we're inclined to prefer Old Westbury. While smaller in extent, it has magnificent allées, several ponds, and a bevy of different special gardens that are a tribute to the taste of Londoner George Crawley, the architect for both mansion and grounds. Planting Fields has naturally rolling terrain, plantings of trees and shrubs that are extensive and varied enough to warrant the *arboretum* label, and of course the famous greenhouses. We'll speak of it next.

Old Westbury Gardens is reached from the Long Island Expressway by leaving it at exit 39, Glen Cove Road, taking the service road east 1.2 miles to Old Westbury Road, and then turning right on it to reach the entrance in .25 mile. It is open Wednesday through Monday from 10:00 A.M. to 5:00 P.M. from late April through October, and also in December for special holiday events in the mansion. There is a $6.00 admission fee to the grounds

OLD WESTBURY GARDENS

Rest Rooms

Walled Garden

Ghost Walk

Pinetum

Bluebell Walk

Rose Garden

Autumn Walk

Wildflower Meadow

Lilac Walk

Temple of Love

Cottage Garden

Demonstration Gardens

Primrose Path

EAST LAKE

Linden Allee

Woodland Walk

Gift Shop

Lake Trail

WEST POND

Shell Mosaic

Mansion

Boxwood Gardens

0   1/10   2/10

Miles

Entrance

Parking Area

Picnic Area and Cafe

N

and a separate $4.00 fee for the mansion tour. For information on the many special events, call 333–0048.

You enter through wrought-iron gates. The grass is tended, and you will not believe the beech and linden trees, which immediately establish an important theme. After parking you can start to encounter the many surprises of the landscaping by embarking on a 1.3-mile self-guided tour that could take two hours. You are gently steered to the boxwood garden, Italianate two-acre walled garden, pinetum, rose garden, Ghost Walk, cottage garden, demonstration garden, woodland walk, and more. You return to the stately Stuart-style mansion after this vista of the gracious living that John S. Phipps and his family enjoyed and encounter the indoor counterpart of their gardens.

When you come into the house, there are fresh flowers in all rooms, and the dinner table is set; it is just as though the Phipps family had stepped out but would be back shortly, as though you were an invited weekend guest. The rooms are pleasant: light, airy, homey, and tastefully decorated by someone with a fine sense of color. Although the home is not ostentatious, it displays evidence of considerable wealth—English antiques; paintings by Reynolds, Raeburn, Gainsborough, Constable, and Sargent; gilded mirrors and crystal chandeliers.

To further the ambience, there is a nice picnic area in the woods with a self-service "Café in the Woods." All in all, it's a place to visit again and again, ever fresh and ever lovely.

PLANTING FIELDS
ARBORETUM

N

Planting Fields Road

Chicken Valley Road

Dwarf Conifer Garden
English Hollies
Rhododendron Species
American Hollies
Heather Garden
Synoptic Garden
Beech Grove
East Lawn
North Rhododendron Park
Parking No. 1
Nature Trail
Parking No. 2
South Rhododendron Park
Bea Jones Garden
Herb Garden
Stable Complex
Arb. Center
Main Greenhouse
Nursery
Maintenance
Rest Rms.
Coe Hall
Camellia Greenhouse
Rose Arbor
Formal Gardens
Perennial Garden
Maple Collection
Carriage House
West Lawn
Magnolia Walk
Conifer Trail
Edwin Costich Memorial Garden
North Country Garden Club Wildflower Walk
Texus Field
Carshalton Gate 1723
Nature Trail
Woodland Trail
Woodland

0   1/10   2/10

Miles

31

Planting Fields Arboretum

Planting Fields Arboretum State Historic Park is one of the best loved places on Long Island's Gold Coast, probably because it appeals to so many interests. The 409 acres of woodlands, rolling lawns and fields, and cultivated gardens provide a wonderful setting for the Tudor-Revival mansion Coe Hall and for a flock of greenhouses and other buildings.

In truth, the mansion and the landscaping compete as equals for the visitor's applause as the most noteworthy sights, thanks to the vision of William Robertson Coe. He bought the lands and the first house on the estate in 1913 and in 1918 began to build the present sixty-five-room mansion in a style of architecture reflecting what was popular during the reign of Queen Elizabeth I. Outstanding craftsmanship and meticulous detailing can be seen in hand-carved chimneys, stonework, and woodwork. The period rooms are fully restored and reflect an age of grace and luxury. Guided tours are available daily April through October, for a $3.50 fee, usually just in the afternoons. There are occasional special events to disturb normal schedules—you can check by calling 922-0479.

For the walker, landscaping rises to the fore. Designed by Frederick Law Olmsted Jr. in the early 1920s, the arboretum offers a spectacular display of trees and shrubs, many imported from abroad. The sweeping lawns boast majestic beech and linden trees, as well as cedar, fir, elm, tulip, maple, holly, oak, and magnolia. Beyond the lawns are native fields and forest, with laurel, rhododendron, and dogwood much in evidence along the drives and trails.

In contrast to the lawns are specialized garden areas and shrub plantings, including rose, dwarf conifer, rhododendron, and synoptic gardens, and extensive annual, perennial, and bulb plantings. Then there are the magnificent Camellia Greenhouse to visit for late-winter beauty and the Main Greenhouse for specialized collections and seasonal displays.

There are many different ways to enjoy Planting Fields, and the simple one of wandering at will across the lawns, through the gardens, and along woodland paths and drives surely makes up for the lack of a specific route or trail for the walker to follow. Practically every area and season has something to offer.

Planting Fields is managed by the New York State Department of Parks and is open every day of the year (except Christmas) from 9:00 A.M. to 5:00 P.M. The greenhouses are open from 10:00 A.M. to 4:00 P.M., and a call to 922–9200 will let you discover what special exhibitions are in progress. Admission to the grounds is $3.00 per car all year on weekends and holidays and also on weekdays between May 1 and Labor Day. Weekdays off-season are free. To reach Planting Fields, turn north off Route 25A, on Wolver Hollow Road, following it until it ends at Chicken Valley Road. Turn right and follow Chicken Valley Road for just over 2 miles and then turn right (shortly after you pass some magnificent English wrought-iron gates) on Planting Fields Road to the entrance.

32

Caumsett State Park

Since 1961, 1,500 acres of the original 1,750-acre estate over-looking Long Island Sound, which made up the fabulous English-style domain of Marshall Field III, has been owned by New York State and is today administered by the Long Island State Park and Recreation Commission. And it is a grand place to walk.

A grand place in every way because there are not apt to be crowds, with the many restrictions—no picnicking facilities (so you must pack in your sandwich, bring your own drinking water, carry away your leftovers), no swimming, no pets, no playgrounds, no camping, no driving beyond the parking area at the park booth, a matter of 2 miles to the Long Island Sound.

This gives Caumsett a wonderfully remote aspect once you walk beyond the marvelous old farm buildings and magnificent stable nearby or down along the shore, so plan to spend the better part of a day. It is open 8:00 A.M. to 4:30 P.M. daily. From Memorial Day through Labor Day there is an entrance fee of $3.00. To get there from Route 25A in Huntington, turn north on West Neck Road to the park, a very pretty 5.5 miles.

It is hard to imagine that one man owned this vast park and that it was a farm that made its own power and was self-sufficient in most every way. Miles of roads were built for motoring and horseback riding. There was tennis, indoors and out, pheasant and skeet shooting, polo, trout fishing, a herd of prize cattle, and

CAUMSETT
STATE PARK

LONG ISLAND SOUND

Marshall
Field
House

1

½

Riding
Stables

0

Dairy
Farm

Miles

Winter
Cottage

Summer Cottage

West Neck /
Lloyd Harbor Road

Park
Entrance

Henry Lloyd
House

LLOYD HARBOR

N

an extensive vegetable garden. None of the buildings is open to the public. They now house the Queens College Center for Environmental Teaching and Research, the BOCES Outdoor and Environmental Education Program, the Caumsett Equestrian Center, et cetera. For further information call 423–1770.

You will find here many specimen trees of interest—beech, oak, pine, dogwood, locust. You will find meadows, a salt marsh, and, below the large terrace of the main house, a pond where various waterfowl may be observed, and also the extensive shoreline along the Sound.

BLYDENBURGH
COUNTY PARK

25A

Caleb Smith
State Park

Jericho Turnpike

New Mill Road

Brookside Drive

N

W

W

Mill

Blydenburgh
House

STUMP
POND

W

W

Croft Lane

Old Willets Path

Brookside Drive

347

Veterans Highway

454

1

½

0
Miles

33

Blydenburgh County Park

East of Old Willets Path, this Suffolk County Park has had a long history with very few owners. In 1798 Isaac Blydenburgh, seeing a good business opportunity, joined with some Smith relatives to buy the 588-acre parcel. They put in the dam that created the pond and erected grist, saw, and fulling mills, which flourished for a long time. Blydenburgh became the sole owner in 1801, erected the present house in 1821, and passed the property on to his heirs. In 1938 the property left the family to become David Weld's estate, and he in turn sold it to the county in 1968.

The park is mostly woodland with swamps and fields, and with Stump Pond, which we understand is second in size on Long Island only to Lake Ronkonkoma. The pond is long and irregularly shaped, somewhat like a boot with a pointed toe. No swimming is permitted, but rowboats are available, so it is a popular fishing place as well as campground. A number of trails and dirt roads make for easy walking; you'll also encounter horseback riders.

The park has two focal points for visitors. One is on the north side of Stump Pond, where the old homestead and mill are located, and the other is at the south end. Both have parking and limited visitor facilities, and they connect with each other by trails along both sides of the lake. The park is open dawn to dusk; the park office is near the south entrance (854–3713). The best way to reach the northern part is from the western edge of

Smithtown Branch on Route 25, Jericho Turnpike. Turn south off the turnpike at the traffic signal at Brooksite Drive and go one block, then west on New Mill Road, which leads directly into the park. The other part is reached from Veterans Highway (Route 454) just across from the road leading to the county buildings south of the highway.

Parking is limited in season to Suffolk County residents with permits. At other times of the year this restriction has not been rigorously enforced, and the chances are that the rangers will treat you with courtesy if you're not a nuisance.

Our suggestion for a good walk here is to follow the trail from the house by the north parking area down to Stump Pond. The trees near the house have all been planted but are native to the area. Once all this was tended farmland, but it was allowed some time ago to go back to nature. Now plants and surrounding shore are slowly filling in the lake, and everywhere is becoming overgrown. The area covered by the lake is 120 acres, and the fish consist of bass, sunfish, bluegills, as well as a few trout. The plants are common water lily and yellow pond lily, as well as water milfoil. You continue on the path southward across the dam by the mill and along the western shores of the lake to the stream, which you follow until the trail splits. Take the one to your left, which crosses the stream and goes up the hill, and then follow it back so that you reach the high bluff of the peninsula from which you see a whole panorama of the lake. The walk to this point is a little over a mile, and if you wish to extend it, you can continue along the fire road toward the southern reaches of the lake.

The trail soon turns away from the lake to come out on Croft Lane. Turn left here and continue on south, passing through a strip of woodland, then going left just north of some county buildings, and downhill to cross a footbridge over the south inlet brook and on to a connection with the east shore trail at the park office. A complete circuit around Stump Pond is a good workout, since it is nearly 5 miles long, but it abounds with lovely views of the lake and its waterfowl.

34

Bayard Cutting Arboretum and Heckscher State Park

Anyone familiar with New York's Central Park knows the genius of Frederick Law Olmsted in grouping trees together. See what he started here on the banks of the Connetquot River on a very rich man's estate in 1887. There are 690 acres with trim lawns and open meadows, a wildflower garden, a marshy refuge, and paths that lead everywhere. Along the river's edge, around and through woods, it is difficult to imagine a nicer walk anywhere or one with a setting more gracious than the one provided for public use here. The estate is maintained by the Long Island State Park and Recreation Commission, given in trust to the state by Mr. Cutting's daughter, though it is not technically a state park. There is no picnicking, but there is a $3.00 per car charge for admission from early April to Labor Day and on weekends only up to mid-November. Hours are 10:00 A.M. to 4:00 P.M. Wednesday through Sunday. Telephone 581-1002.

To reach the arboretum, take Southern State Parkway to Heckscher Parkway. Leave it at exit 45E and follow the signs east along Montauk Highway (Route 27A).

There are five different trails laid out and marked, each with different colors, and were you to take the allotted time on each, the total time suggested would be three and a half hours. We

BAYARD CUTTING
ARBORETUM

27

Sunrise Highway

W

WEST BROOK

L.I.R.R.

W

Entrance

CONNETQUOT RIVER

Union Blvd.

Montauk Highway

W

27A

Mansion

N

½

¼

0

Miles

recommend that you plan to spend at least two and a half hours here and make a most pleasant morning or afternoon of it by combining two or more of these walks into one longer one.

There is also a seasonal aspect to consider in planning your walk here. Wildflowers should be out in late March and April, rhododendrons in late May and June. Changing colors are engaging in October. Even on a hot summer's day, however, the welcome release is here; a cooling breeze off the river, shade from the mature trees, and benches conveniently at hand will probably quietly lure you to sit a spell.

The rambly, old, informal house is maintained in good repair and partially open. Tea and simple snacks are available in season, cafeteria style, and tables on the large enclosed porch looking out over the river offer an attractive setting for a relaxing break. A fine collection of stuffed birds and Indian artifacts is on display and should be recommended to visitors.

Heckscher State Park does not offer much in the way of discovery, and so we wouldn't especially recommend it. The Long Island Greenbelt Trail, however, starts there at the east end of parking field 8 on the edge of Great South Bay. (If field 8 is closed use the unnumbered field to the west of it. There is a concrete walkway connecting these two fields.) It can provide a pleasant shore, meadow, and woods walk for whatever distance time and energy permit. In fact, after about 4 miles it passes "just across the road" from the entrance to the arboretum.

Heckscher Park is heavily used in the summertime, but its nearly 1,700 acres can soak up a lot of people, and with the usual cool on-shore breeze from the bay, it can still be a lovely place. There are wildflowers in the wetlands and meadows in the spring, and in the fall Monarch butterflies pass through in great numbers as they migrate south. The park is open daily from 8:00 A.M. to sunset and is reached simply by following the Heckscher Parkway extension of Southern State Parkway to the end. In the summer months there is a $3.00 or $4.00 charge per car, depending on whether or not the swimming pool is open.

Marshes, Creeks, and Bogs

These aren't necessarily walks where you'll need your rubber footgear, but water figures prominently in each. It may be a lake or marsh that is full of birds to be observed; It may be a brook or nascent river heading for the sea with a trail beside it that leads you through lush undergrowth or giant trees. In any case there will be a lot more visible life here than is common in the drier woodland walks. That of course carries with it the prospect of mosquitoes in season and muddy spots on the trails here and there. We've found these drawbacks unimportant compared to the larger pleasures of these walks.

These wetlands, and of course the ocean and sound beaches, reveal the great variety of natural beauty that has escaped the pressures of urban sprawl, the places where the ibis feeds in the salt marshes, where the beach plum covers the dunes with her spring blossoms, and the woodcock starts up from the cattails. These walks particularly call for you to bring along your binoculars and to proceed quietly along the paths.

Three of these walks are in very close proximity to "civilization," one being noisily close to Kennedy airport and the others only a few hundred feet from solid residential areas, but you'll find it easy to ignore the man-made noises and concentrate on the natural world. The birds and small animals are clearly undisturbed by their urban surroundings, and so can we be.

Another point to be made is that these walks may surprise you with the great numbers of waterfowl that now winter here, as compared to a few decades ago. Canada geese are especially common; at times it almost seems as though they have become permanent residents, not just visitors on their way south or north, and indeed many do stay year-round.

Shu Swamp Preserve

JAMAICA BAY
WILDLIFE REFUGE

GRASSY
BAY

EAST
POND

Cross Bay Boulevard

N

JACKS
HOLE
CREEK

WEST
POND

IND Subway

Visitor
Center

BLACK WALL CHANNEL

0   ¼   ½

Miles

Broad
Channel

35

Jamaica Bay Wildlife Refuge

The sun sets in a splash of color behind the towers of the city. A jumbo jet floats silently into Kennedy on the other side of the bay. And West Pond at Jamaica Bay's Wildlife Refuge is alive, teeming with swooping terns, black skimmers seining their dinners through their amazing red bills, plovers and phalaropes skittering about in the shallows, the great egret and great blue heron standing, majestic in the tall reeds. This is late afternoon in early August. The juxtaposition here of what man hath wrought in the distance with the magnificence of nature in the foreground calls attention strikingly to the question of whether we can keep a balance between these sometimes inimical forces.

You need a permit to visit the refuge, but one is available (free) at the front desk of the visitor's center, which is open daily 8:30 A.M. to 5:00 P.M., except on Thanksgiving, Christmas, and New Year's. The refuge is now a part of Gateway National Recreation Area and hence the National Park system.

If you care to drive (Belt Parkway to exit 17S, then turn south on Cross Bay Boulevard), there is a visitor parking lot on the west side of Cross Bay Boulevard 1.4 miles south of the first bridge. Look for the one discreet sign. Or you can come by subway. The IND Far Rockaway A or H train takes you there (Broad Channel stop). In case you do, walk back 1 mile to the entrance.

But don't be put off by a series of shack dwellings cheek by jowl on the edges of the bay, sitting upon tenuous foundations. This walk is incidental.

The refuge itself comprises approximately 14.5 square miles, much of it islands and tidal marshes. The accessible spot is the West Pond region, and West Pond is a forty-five-acre freshwater pond with a fine 1.5 mile trail around it. A first trip to the Jamaica Bay Refuge is inspiring, especially undertaken at sunrise or sunset. Those responsible for seeing the possibilities, creating here a forever wild area available to birds on the Atlantic flyway and people via the subway, deserve highest praise and homage. Sit on one of the benches and turn your glasses or scope on these creatures. Many will use Jamaica Bay as a regular stopover during spring or fall migrations. Maybe as you sit here, the short-eared owl will rise from the grasses and swoop about on his nocturnal search for a mouse or two. Even if you don't know one bird from another, the whole setting will impress you.

There are a few suggestions we'd make for enhancing your enjoyment here. Bring along your bird book and binoculars and, if it's a buggy time of year, your favorite insect repellent. Although there's usually a breeze and the bugs may not bother you, in some grassy protected areas, you may wish you had brought it along. Also, eat before you come. There are several picnic tables available outside the visitor center—which is the *only* area for picnicking, and there is no place to dine nearby.

Across on the east side of the road there is another, larger section of the refuge with a one-hundred-acre pond and shoreline on the bay as well. Sometimes rare birds stop here, and you may want to look in, if you have strength after you walk around West Pond. If so, check first with the visitor center for trail conditions.

Please remember that all the vegetation makes a fine habitat for ticks and poison ivy, so take proper precautions against both.

The mailing address for information is Jamaica Bay Wildlife Refuge, Gateway NRA, Floyd Bennett Field, Brooklyn, NY 11234; (718) 318–4340.

36

John F. Kennedy Memorial Wildlife Sanctuary

As you fly into Kennedy Airport, you realize that the surrounding area is a vast network of tidal marshes, low-lying islands like lily pads in the bay, and barrier beaches conspicuously uninhabited by man, which causes us to speculate on wildlife there. Knowing that the sea rising over a marsh floods this land with chemical riches, that the ocean moderates temperatures here, and that wildlife in wetlands is abundant, we are intrigued by the thousands of acres behind Jones and Tobay beaches. So if you speculate about this as we do, then we must recommend to you the John F. Kennedy Memorial Wildlife Sanctuary.

It is a 500-acre stretch, swallowed up by more than 5,000 acres owned by Oyster Bay Town and managed by the New York State Conservation Department, but it provides an opportunity to investigate something of what wetlands life is about. You must obtain a permit to visit the sanctuary by going to the Oyster Bay Town Hall South, 977 Hicksville Road, Massapequa (1 block south of the Jerusalem Avenue intersection). Find the "Beaches" sections of the Parks Department and fill out a permit request form, and after a week or so the permit will be mailed to you. No wonder Long Island has high taxes and unhappy taxpayers! Office hours are 9:00 A.M. to 4:30 P.M. daily; telephone number is 797–4110.

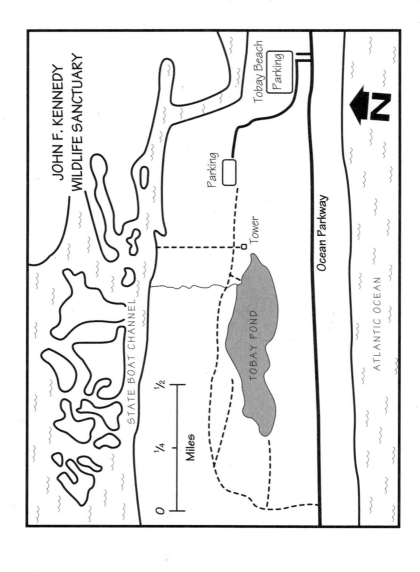

When you do have your permit, get on the Ocean Parkway and go east about 4 miles from the Jones Beach traffic circle to the Tobay Beach parking lot (just east of parking area 9). Drive west along the south border of the lot and along a road to the parking area provided for the sanctuary.

There is an old road, over a mile long, which leads through the middle of the area and provides good footing, although absolutely flat and unspectacular because it is bordered by plants growing to a height just over your head, the usual variety of beach and swamp growth. You can leave the road in several places and walk to blinds or to the observation tower from which you can sweep your glasses over the pond and the treetops, but you cannot get much closer on foot to the water.

It was after Labor Day when we walked here, spent a longer time and walked farther than we intended, and were exhausted. From the tower we had watched a large brown female marsh hawk for some time, quartering low over the marshes, its white rump patch marking distinctly visible, its buoyant, tilting glide a joy to observe. There were clouds of tree swallows swooping about and low cherry trees alive with cedar waxwings. We thought we saw a prothonotary warbler. Glossy ibis flew purposefully overhead. Duck arrived at the pond, skidding in for a landing. Kingbirds and white egrets were common, heron and belted kingfishers scarce.

The black-and-orange monarch butterflies were assembled in spectacular concentrations. These frail insects are noted for the long treks they make on their annual mass migrations and all morning continuously called attention to their flutterings.

Bayberry bushes were heavy with fruit; catbrier was in tangles. We noticed that birds had eaten the berries from the pokeweed. When we stretched out to rest on the white sandy dunes that overlook the pond from the northwest, we looked up at a sky everywhere interrupted by winged creatures.

TACKAPAUSHA PRESERVE

L.I.R.R.

Sunrise Highway

27

Washington Avenue

Riverside Avenue

Seaford Avenue

3/10

2/10

1/10

0
Miles

★

Museum

Merrick Road

27A

Southern Section

Jerusalem Avenue

N

4/10

3/10

2/10

1/10

0
Miles

Lakeview Avenue

Seaford Avenue

Clarke Street

Park Drive

Riverside Avenue

Sunrise Highway

Central &
Northern Sections

37

Tackapausha Preserve

This surprising preserve encompasses eighty acres and a fine small museum in the middle of suburbia. A visit provides a pleasant contrast to the surrounding bustle and noise of this heavily developed area. The preserve is essentially a 1.5-mile-long and 1,000-foot-wide strip of woodland surrounding a fresh water stream (Seaford Creek) as it runs south toward the bay. It has three sections, separated by Clark Street and Sunrise Highway (Route 27), with the southern one, where the museum stands, starting just north of Merrick Road on Washington Avenue. Trails run along each side of the brook, so one can easily get up to a 3.5-mile loop walk if desired. Also, for the ambitious, there is a blazed link between these trails and the trails of Massapequa Preserve; it runs along the north side of Sunrise Highway.

Because the stream meanders and branches, there are lots of marshy areas and little ponds along the way, and to the sides there are taller trees. In the southern part you'll see white oak, red maple, and one of the very few remaining stands of Atlantic white cedar on Long Island. There are shadbush, spicebush, and highbush blueberry. On the ground you'll see fern, and in spring, flowers, such as wood anemone and pink lady's slipper.

Because of the variety of plants and insects, there are many different birds at any time of the year. A pamphlet listing nearly

200 species and times of year when you might expect to see them is available at the museum.

The central section comprises fifteen acres and a pond where mallards, green herons, and other water birds can be found. The northern section's forty-five acres is mostly a maple and oak forest, since it is higher and better drained, with wildflowers common in the open areas.

The museum building is a division of the Nassau County Museum of Natural History and well worth a visit. Inside there are informative displays, literature, and usually a nature film to see. Behind it there's a small menagerie with Long Island wildlife, allowing you a good close look at a red-tailed hawk, for instance. The museum is open Tuesday through Saturday 10:00 A.M. to 4:00 P.M., and Sunday 1:00 to 4:00 P.M., with a $1.00 admission fee for adults. The preserve, however, is open dawn to dusk. If you have questions, call 571–7443.

The name Tackapausha, incidentally, is preserved on the original deed for the land in Hempstead. Tackapausha was one of the sachems who agreed to the transfer of land to the early settlers. And that's all we know about him.

Massapequa Preserve

Like the Tackapausha Preserve, this has three sections: southern (Merrick Road to Sunrise Highway), central (to Clark Boulevard), and northern (to Linden Street). It is a quiet place in the midst of superhighways and dense population that offers a pleasant walk of a couple of miles up and back. A crystal-clear stream flowed freshly when we walked here; some kids fished at one of the dams, and two boys had a little rubber raft in the stream. The Massapequa Preserve is a wooded strip, drained by a stream dammed in a couple of places, thus making rather weedy ponds, excellent cover for ducks. The walking is chiefly along a paved bicycle path that runs along the stream, although there are paths into the woods and around ponds. In August the fragrance of sweet pepperbush permeated the air. We watched a least tern hover and dip over a pond, slamming into the water to capture a tiny minnow, and a family of black ducks float secretively through the reeds. Deep rose petals of the rose-mallow flowers, with their bright yellow centers, made a handsome display along the edge of the stream.

For an extended walk, park by Massapequa Lake at Merrick Road and follow the white-blazed Nassau-Suffolk Greenbelt Trail from its beginning there north to Sunrise Highway and on to Clark Boulevard. From there on in the northern part you'll have a choice of the Greenbelt on the west side of the brook or the

MASSAPEQUA PRESERVE

paved bicycle path on the east most of the way up to Linden Street. Parking is possible almost anywhere on Parkside Boulevard or Lake Shore Drive.

If you're really ambitious, you can follow the Greenbelt up to Bethpage State Park (about 6 miles) or all the way to Stillwell Woods and Cold Spring Harbor on the North Shore. The whole 22-mile stretch is best taken in easy stages!

In summer and in migration times, Massapequa Lake will usually have ospreys in evidence, and in winter a great variety of ducks (canvasback, coot, ruddy, etc.) will be at home. Other areas along the stream will reward you with whorled pogonia, white-fringed orchis, sundews, and more. The whole complex provides scarce habitat for many species and green space for people, making ecologists and nature enthusiasts rejoice. Similar areas can be found all along this south side of the glacial outwash plain.

Like Tackapausha, Massapequa Preserve is nominally open dawn to dusk.

SHU SWAMP SANCTUARY

MILL NECK BAY

N

Cleft Road

BEAVER LAKE

Frost Mill Road

Long Island R. R.

Mill Neck R.R. Station

Cocks Lane

Oyster Bay Road

BEAVER BROOK

0   1/10   2/10   3/10   4/10

Miles

39

Shu Swamp Sanctuary

Shu Swamp Sanctuary is the jewel of the several properties owned and managed in the Mill Neck/Locust Valley area by the North Shore Wildlife Sanctuary, Inc. Tracing its origins back to 1929, Shu Swamp is a small but beautiful preserve featuring both wetlands and uplands, with most of the wildlife drawn there by the clear waters of Beaver Brook as it flows through. It's a lovely place to walk, passing on both sides of the marshy estuary that is filled with birds and magnificent trees.

One thing we must stress—wildlife preserves are not recreation areas, so that while visitors are welcome during daylight hours all year, they are asked to observe the posted rules, which forbid fires, camping, picnics, dogs, or any conduct not in keeping with the purposes for which these sanctuaries were established.

The sanctuary is open daily, except Friday, between 7:00 A.M. and 7:00 P.M. from April to October, and 7:00 A.M. to 5:00 P.M. from November through March. Note that the parking area is locked after hours, and parking along the road guarantees a ticket. A full-time warden, Mr. Robert Hornosky, is in charge. The address is P.O. Box 214, Mill Neck, NY 11765; 671–0283. To reach the parking area, turn north off Route 25A on Wolver Hollow Road and follow it until it ends at Chicken Valley Road. Go right and continue 1.6 miles to Frost Mill Road. It leads right, bends left, and continues north to a viaduct over which the Long Island Rail Road tracks cross. The sanctuary parking area is just to the south of the tracks and west of Frost Mill Road. Incidentally, it is just a short walk from the Mill Neck railroad station.

We are prompted to write a few words about the tulip tree because the magnificent stand of tulip trees here along estuarial waters is inspiring, towering as they do probably 100 feet high, their trunks tall and straight and branchless for the first 50 or 60 feet. Considered the handsomest eastern forest tree because of its upright trunk and perfect symmetry, the tulip tree is frequently seen as an ornamental and is scattered throughout Long Island. However, the stand here is rare, perhaps unique, in number of trees well over 150 years old. Their old bark is rich brown and deeply fissured, and some must have diameters of 4 feet or more. Another name by which this tree is known is canoe tree, because the Native Americans made their dugouts from them, and when the English settlers first arrived they found the natives traveling all about Long Island in them. Surrounded by these ancient trees, looking up at those towering trunks, you may see how this was possible—though without modern tools, it took great ingenuity and patience, skill with fire, and endless hours to fashion a seagoing craft of one. These trees give you reason to gasp and to consider the wonder of it all.

The North Shore Wildlife Sanctuary, Inc., is, like The Nature Conservancy, a private organization, grateful for your financial help, and contributions are tax deductible.

40

Peconic River

South of the Middle Country Road (Route 25) and west of Calverton is a large, sparsely populated area, mostly woodlands, with a series of ponds that form the stream that meanders to Riverhead, making the Peconic River the longest on Long Island. It is Robert Cushman Murphy County Park, a long, narrow strip of land on which Horn, Round, Peasys, Woodchoppers, Duck, Sandy, Grassy, Twin, and Jones ponds follow one after another north to south. There are many sandy woods roads in this undeveloped area that make for pleasant walking, but there are so many such roads and trails that you need to pay close attention to your route so as not to get misplaced. The best map available is the one featuring the Long Island Pine Barrens Trail—West Section. (See the comments on this subject for Walk 23.) You can go safely any time of year, except during the winter hunting season. Call the New York State Department of Environmental Conservation at 444–0310 for the exact dates of the open season, and to get the required permit.

This area supports considerable wildlife. Deer are plentiful, and bird life abounds. We have seen at least twenty different mushroom species over the years. (Although we have rushed home afterward to look in our mushroom guide, we have never done more than photograph them.) The great blue heron lives in Woodchoppers Pond. You will see several species of duck, little

PECONIC RIVER

Middle Country Road

25

Robert Cushman
Murphy
County Park

HORN
POND

Swan Pond Road

ROUND
POND

PEASYS
POND

N

WOODCHOPPERS
POND

DUCK
POND

SANDY
POND

Wading River – Manor Road

Y

W

W

25

GRASSY
POND

W

Schultz Road

TWIN
PONDS

W

½

¼

JONE'S
POND

W

0

Miles

W=Pine Barrens Trail

green heron, a Canada goose family, and, in the spring, warblers, the oriole, the scarlet tanager, partridge, and woodcock. We were thrilled to see the rare red crossbill among the pitch pine and oak. The shores of the ponds are marshy, and in the fall the colors are riotous. During rainy periods the trail can be wet in spots.

The half day or more you spend in this area will be peaceful—maybe a fisherman will be here, but we have met only one other hiker in the woods though we have walked here many times.

A good access to these boggy ponds is an unmarked road 2.3 miles north of Long Island Expressway exit 69 on Wading River/Schultz Road or 1.2 miles south on Wading River/Schultz Road from Route 25 and just opposite Wading River–Manor Road. It is a gated dirt road, with only informal provisions for parking on either side, near the posted signs reading COOPERATIVE HUNTING AREA. Another dirt road entry is on Middle Country Road, directly opposite a paved road named Panamoka Trail. Since the Pine Barrens Trail also cuts through this area, it could be used for access, starting at other road crossings.

CRANBERRY BOG

L.I.R.R.

RIVERHEAD

25

94

PECONIC RIVER

24

24

County
Center

LITTLE RIVER

CEDAR POND

Swamp

Swamp

Cranberry Bogs

63

SWEEZY POND

51

Moriches Road

Lakeside Drive

WILDWOOD LAKE

N

1

½

0

Miles

Cranberry Bog

A rather large area of county-owned land right in Riverhead is a 211-acre former cranberry bog. It is a unique haven for plant and animal life, probably the only remaining habitat of this type remaining on Long Island. Although it is unmarked, it is a favorite haunt of naturalists, and has an interesting history.

In the early 1800s the Peconic River was in demand as a source of water power for mill wheels, but after the Civil War coal and other fuels took over, and the water was no longer needed as much. Someone had the sensible idea of using these lowlands and the abundant water for raising cranberries, and the resulting industry flourished from about 1875 to the 1930s, at one point becoming the third largest producers of cranberries in the country. These small bogs could not compete with the major growers elsewhere, however; operating costs rose, and in 1959 a major pesticide used on cranberries gave the death blow by turning out to be carcinogenic.

This area is now held by Suffolk County as a preserve and nature-oriented park for its residents. An environmental staff oversees the preserve, but it is open for nature walks on an informal basis.

To find it, drive south on Route 63, which leads from Riverhead Circle toward Wildwood Lake. There are no signs, but there is a chain-link gate at the service road on your right, just after

Lakeside Drive, which veers off to the left. There is space to park a few cars.

Although the park gate is usually closed, there are a few unmarked trails, and you won't have any trouble walking around the gate. It is a place that makes a fascinating ramble. A bridge has recently been completed over the Little River, and it is now possible to make a loop around Sweezy Pond. The old cranberry fields lie to the east of the pond, and dikes permit you to penetrate some of the jungly growth. We say it is a ramble because to enjoy this spot is to explore, walking here and there along fringes of the wetlands. But we implore you: Walk quietly and cautiously, respecting stillness and wildlife. Deer and heron, swan and geese as well as duck, live here, so try especially hard not to disturb. The variety of shrub and ground cover is extraordinary—sweet pepperbush, bayberry, beach plum, wild grape, bearberry, cranberry, bear oak, so many bog plants—and the pond is full of water lilies, slender arrowhead, and reed, a catalog of freshwater swamplands growth. If you like this kind of exploring, you should enjoy a leisurely stroll here.

Incidentally, there is another series of old cranberry bogs nearby that are worth visiting. Referring to the Walk 40 map, take Wading River–Manor Road southeast from its junction with Schultz Road 1.1 miles to Old River Road (left). Proceed for about 1 mile on Old River Road to its junction with River Road. The bogs run both north and south from this point along a small stream that drains Swan Pond into the Peconic River. It's a pleasant area, often frequented by deer that come to drink from the stream.

42

Quogue Wildlife Refuge

The New York State Department of Environmental Conservation has had, since 1952, a long-term lease to manage this refuge, a 200-acre parcel that is headwaters and drainage basin of the Quantuck Creek. This provides varied wetlands—swamp, freshwater bog, pot holes, and ponds as well as a tidal estuary. Also there are dwarf pine barrens up at the north end. Altogether there are 8 miles of trails. The details of the way the place has developed suggest talented and dedicated professional guidance. The sanctuary lies just north of the railroad tracks above the village of Quogue on Old Country Road, which runs north of the Montauk Highway and makes its way around into the Quogue-Riverhead Road. Their phone number is 653–4771.

As you come into the preserve there is a pen complex where a talking crow welcomes you, and there are other examples of local animals. Nearby, in a fenced area, are some deer; and wild turkey roam at will in the open foraging area. There are several tall martin houses. The large pond just at the entrance has a permanent resident fleet of Canada geese and varieties of ducks and waterfowl seasonally.

In spring Canada geese families go about training their young, parading in the grass, one parent ahead and one behind, and the little flock between. Somehow they find the living so good here they stay.

QUOGUE WILDLIFE
REFUGE

N

½

¼

0
Miles

QUANTUCK CREEK

Quogue-Riverhead Road

104

Old Country Road

L.I.R.R.

South Country Road

Old Main Road

Walking is clear-cut. You can take the path that goes around the pond about .7 mile or the one that follows the perimeter of the refuge for more than 2 miles. We often decide to do both. Wherever you go, you will see typical flora of the Long Island pine barrens, oak and pine interspersed with various berry bushes birds like to feed on. The ground cover is bearberry and blueberry, and there are black cherry, beach plum, and shadbush, as well as nearly seventy varieties of wildflowers. One summer we were delighted to find in a boggy spot a small stand of the exquisite, tiny, white-blossomed bog orchid.

There are a number of places to sit and quietly observe, whichever path you take. Very often, on the ice pond on the north, there'll be a little green heron or some mallards. You can explore this refuge with no fear of getting lost. It is open daily from 8:00 A.M. to dusk.

Sand Spits and Points

We've separated these walks from the sections devoted to Long Island's long, sandy shorelines, both north and south, mostly as a matter of convenience. These geographic features have the same water boundaries as the beaches and share the same varieties of vegetation and wildlife. Still, they are different in outlook, for most face land not very far off, most have calmer waters, and they just seem to have a different atmosphere.

One walk (Morton Refuge) is really practical only in the fall and winter as ospreys, piping plovers, and colonies of terns nest there from April through August. The nesting areas are normally fenced off at that time to prevent people from disturbing these endangered birds.

The walks we've listed here all permit fairly extensive walking along the shoreline, though not as much as the beach walks. They remind us, though, that there are literally dozens of places where you can gain access to a calm shoreline, like these, in the off seasons. These are the town and county beaches that provide recreation along Great South Bay, the north shore harbors, and the beaches along Peconic and Gardiners bays. Other points of access are public roads that run right down to the water's edge. Usually there are parking restrictions, but off-season, and with local inquiry, you should be able to find many such places to walk.

Montauk Point, of course, is the one place that is fully exposed to the open Atlantic, and while it is often tranquil there, the steady erosion that is threatening the lighthouse tells of violent wave action at almost any time of the year. Also, in contrast to the other spots, Montauk has a quite extensive trail network inland from the beach that is worth exploring.

Jessup Neck, Morton National Wildlife Refuge

MORTON NATIONAL
WILDLIFE REFUGE

NOYACK
BAY

LITTLE PECONIC
BAY

N

1

½

0

Miles

NOYACK CREEK

Clam
Island

38

Noyac Road

43

Morton National Wildlife Refuge

Dividing Little Peconic Bay and Noyack Bay, jutting out from the north shore of the south fork of the island, just above Watermill, is Jessup's Neck. Of the numerous points, necks, and promontories that extend into the waters surrounding Long Island, this offers a wide variety of terrains, and walking here is great for many reasons. It is the Elizabeth Alexandra Morton Wildlife Refuge and is managed by the U.S. Government Fish and Wildlife Service as a resting and feeding area for migratory birds. The locked gate is open from sunrise till sunset.

The office (725–2270) is in the little building to the right beyond the parking area, and you may find one of the staff there. Walking, you can spend an hour or a day, come back again and again, and never tire of the combination of beach, pond, woods, and wetlands here.

The refuge is most easily reached by leaving Montauk Highway (Route 27) on Deerfield Road about 0.4 mile east of Water Mill, and heading north on it until you reach Noyac Road. Turn right on it and in about a half mile you'll reach the refuge. Drive into the grounds through a gate on the northern side of Noyac Road; park here near an old barn a few hundred yards beyond. Stop at the kiosk, which has a map and pictures, for a leaflet about the refuge.

The path down to the bay is about a half mile and planted with many kinds of berry bushes—delectables for the land birds who frequent this quiet sanctuary. There is honeysuckle, myrtle, and rural charm. Be quiet and alert. We have come down this path on an early evening and surprised a graceful doe feasting on these same bushes. The path emerges upon a long narrow strip of beach on the bay with a small inlet from Noyack Bay on the right. This area supports some 500 black duck who winter here, as well as a variety of other water birds all year.

Now and then a clammer in the inlet leans out of his boat to scoop the bottom with his clamming rake. In fall or winter you'll see scallop boats in the bay dragging, though these juicy morsels are dwindling alarmingly, and nowhere else in the world does such a tiny, sweet, tender scallop exist.

The neck beyond this point is a closed area from April 1 to August 15, so as to leave the ospreys, piping plovers, and least terns that nest here quite undisturbed. There is one active osprey nest near the far end of the inlet lagoon that you can easily see even in the closed season. As for the rest of the peninsula, plan on visiting it in fall and winter only. When you can walk there, in about a mile and a half you will come to a sharp rise and spread of land on a wooded promontory. We like to walk in the woods on the path and then return by the beach. At the beginning of the wooded path there was once a farmhouse. In the spring a carpet of daffodils appears out of the myrtle, splendid in color in this secluded habitat.

In the spring woods, during the warbler migration you see some fifteen different varieties flitting among the big oaks before the leaves come out. And down on the beach to the west of the neck, look out to the fish weir where ospreys and cormorants often sit on poles where the pickings are concentrated.

The Morton Refuge can be a cool and refreshing place in summer, when the afternoon breeze from the southwest whistles across the neck. In winter, when the bay freezes solid, if the winds across the ice are too chilling, there are many protected areas of woodland to the east before you reach the bay, and calm shelter for a walk under cover. One early spring we discovered a strangely eerie sight of dry white bones in a bed of greenest myrtle, the carcass of a deer dead of starvation or exhaustion. Later the refuge manager told us he had taken the skeleton to a school for preservation.

When you leave the parking area, you will quickly see a path leading right. This is a loop trail about 0.4 mile long that winds past a pond and through woods (devastated by Hurricane Bob in 1991) to rejoin the main trail about halfway to the beach.

Incidentally, this is one of over 500 refuges managed by the Fish and Wildlife Service throughout the United States—many of them provide similar opportunities for walking and observing wildlife.

CEDAR POINT
COUNTY PARK

← half mile
to point

CEDAR
POND

Bluff

NORTHWEST
HARBOR

ALEWIVE POND

Nature Trail

Office

N

1

3/4

1/2

1/4

0
Miles

Alewive Brook Road

Northwest Road

44

Cedar Point County Park

In the town of East Hampton, 6.5 miles directly north of Georgica, occupying one of the many peninsulas that jut into Gardiner's Bay and give this area such meandering shapes, is Cedar Point, a choice park of 600 acres. This is a Suffolk County park, and you will find parking space here, as in all Suffolk County parks, limited to Suffolk County residents with permits. Trails are not heavy traffic areas, and hikers are not discouraged. For information, call 852–7620.

To find the park entrance if you're headed east on the Montauk Highway (Route 27), slow down as you pass the East Hampton Airport. The road signs were not made to be read while traveling 40 miles per hour. Turn north on the first road past the airport, Stephen Hands Path. Continue on it 2 miles, across Route 114; it connects with Old Northwest Road, which bears off to the left. Continue on this for 1.8 miles to a fork, where you go right on Northwest Road 1.7 miles to the crossing with Alewive Brook Road. Jog left and enter the park there to the north. Or, driving from East Hampton, follow Three Mile Harbor Road and turn left on Springy Banks Road, which also runs into Alewive Brook Road.

You enter the Northwest Woods, a high bluff generally 50 feet above the waters of Gardiners Bay to the north, and drop down alongside Alewive Pond to Cedar Pond, beyond where you'll find a camping and parking area. There are deer in these woods; look sharply in the late afternoon. When you park, you can walk out on the spit, which points west. It's a fine walk, with a striking granite lighthouse at the tip. And though surely you may temporarily lose your sense of direction, you'll look south onto Northwest Harbor and Barcelona Point, northwest onto Shelter Island, north onto Orient Beach State Park, and east onto Gardiners Island; eventually the geography of these fingers and watery shores will sort itself out.

There's a good nature trail (leaflets available) running from the park office area opposite Alewive Pond 0.7 mile out to an observation platform at the top of the bluffs overlooking Gardiners Bay. On a clear day you should easily see the Connecticut shore 15 miles away beyond Orient Point.

The walk west to Cedar Point is just over a mile. The inner shore is sandy, the outer one pebbly. From this entry east along a stretch of wild beaches to Lafarges Landing is a distance of 2 miles. Whichever way you choose to go will be delightful, particularly in early spring or fall—summer afternoons can be crowded. Jingle shells, scallop shells, boat shells, or slipper shells and pear-shaped whelks are nature's handiworks you'll find here, along with all the other flotsam that give beachcombing variety.

The Park is open all year, basically from 8:00 A.M. to dusk. That means the gates close about 4:00 P.M. from November through February.

45

Northwest Creek

Northwest Creek (Northwest Harbor County Park) is protected all around by the county as an undeveloped nature preserve of approximately 337 acres. Though it does not offer miles of trails, we find it an attractive place to park and poke around on foot. The creek oozes out of a swamp, spreads out into prime Long Island wetland, and at its mouth forms a lovely secluded pool of a harbor protected by a sand spit from wind and waves offshore.

You drive on to a large parking area near the harbor where fishermen launch their flat-bottomed boats to venture out into the harbor or sound or bay beyond.

On the left the creek fingers deep into a marsh. When we first came upon this out-of-the-way place, a lady came up to us as we were looking through our field glasses and asked if we had seen her ospreys. It was early April, and she said they were back again, pointing to a tree on the border of the wood at the edge of the marsh and saying that their nest had been knocked off the platform, but that she was hoping they would build again soon. At that time we had never had a close look at one of these magnificent hawks, so we shared her excitement.

On the right is the spit of land that reaches around the harbor, and we find it a beautiful place to walk. Because of what is underfoot, it sets you thinking about primeval beginnings. In stacks of dried sea grasses are carapaces of many horseshoe

NORTHWEST CREEK

NORTHWEST HARBOR

Barcelona
Point

NORTHWEST CREEK

Northwest Harbor County Park

Swamp Road

Northwest Landing Road

Mile Hill Road

Old Northwest Road

N

0   ¼   ½

Miles

crabs, the tiniest not much bigger than your thumb, left behind by moulting crabs. Actually the horseshoe is not a crab at all but of the same family as the spider, a living fossil whose relatives became extinct 400 million years ago. Then the fiddler crab burrows here in the moist sand among the reeds. Neat little balls of sand piled meticulously beside his burrow look as though he had a machine to turn them out exactly calibrated. At low tide it is clear that the marsh is groaning with abundant nourishment for birds and fish.

There is really no particular path to follow to the bay here; step wherever you can. An old pair of sneakers is the best footgear because although the ground is damp, it isn't necessary to wade. The beach proper is narrow with an array of scallop shells that sea gulls drop. Often the whole operation is so neat that the two parts of the shell are still together after the gull has extracted his dinner. At the east end the beach is low with tidal pools, but as you walk westward toward the inlet and Barcelona Point, the dunes get higher, perhaps put there when they dredged the inlet after a storm. You can walk all the way around the edge of the beach and back to the little harbor, making an elongated circle. The preserve supports a great variety of local wildlife, and naturalists have observed, among other birds, marsh hawks, screech owls, warblers, and thrashers. It is a relatively undisturbed treasure trove of the things Rachel Carson talks about so eloquently in her book *The Edge of the Sea*.

To get to Northwest Creek, turn north off Montauk Highway (Route 27) on Stephen Hands Path at Georgica, then follow Old Northwest Road through twists and turns 1.8 miles to a fork, where you bear left to reach Northwest Landing Road. Follow it left for about 0.5 mile to the end. As an alternative, take Route 114 southeast from Sag Harbor for about 2 miles, then turn left on Swamp Road. Follow it until you come to Northwest Landing Road.

Eagle Point

HALLOCK BAY

★

○

Browns Point

Peters Neck Point

GARDINERS BAY

1

½

0
Miles

ORIENT HARBOR

□ Lighthouse

ORIENT BEACH
STATE PARK

46

Orient Beach State Park

At the end of Route 25 on the north fork of Long Island, just before you get to the water and the ferry to New London, on your right is the usual rustic state park sign for Orient Beach—but Orient Beach is not a usual state park. Turn and drive along the causeway to the parking lot. If it's spring or early summer, look to your right as you go along the causeway for the osprey nest across the water. A faithful pair returns yearly, and they are magnificent birds, these fish hawks. Sometimes you can watch them fish, diving from on high and catching a fish as much as 10 feet below the surface with their talons.

The park (323–2440) is open daily all year, 8:00 A.M. to 4:30 P.M. October through May, 8:00 A.M. to 6:00 P.M. in June and September, and 8:00 A.M. to 8:00 P.M. in July and August. The parking fee is $4.00 in July and August and $3.00 in June. After 4:00 P.M. there is never a charge. The summer months are the most crowded time and not one we particularly recommend because when you walk from the parking lot out onto the beach and turn to your right, you'll find it is a favorite picnicking and swimming spot. One-hundred yards past the lifeguard, however, you escape the bulk of the crowd. As you move around the curve of the beach, you have the choice of keeping to the edge of the water or following the jeep tracks into the interior of this spit. You may be confused because Orient Point looks to the northeast, but this narrow strip of land that is Orient Beach, 4 miles long, runs to the southwest.

What makes it unusual? It affords beautiful views of Gardiners Bay and its shores and islands. Wander at will among the scrub pine, for you are never far from salt water on either side. There are two ponds in the interior that attract water birds, and here among the stunted pines and wetlands there is a herd of deer that comes and goes to the mainland. Although we have seen their tracks many times, we have actually seen the deer only fleetingly in winter. You cannot be quiet enough to surprise these wily, graceful creatures, but how they can conceal themselves in this narrow quarter is a mystery. They blend in and get lost as nature intended.

A good plan is to go out by the beach, pebbly but not bad footing, and back through the interior. If you get as far as the tip, you will come close to the recently and handsomely rebuilt Long Beach Bar Light (locally called the "Bug" Light), whose predecessors guided fishing boats into Greenport.

The place is out of this world. On a February 6th, when we walked out to the point, the sky was clear and the Apollo 14 mission had landed on the moon. The refreshment building was boarded up (now it's open all year), and the ground was frozen. The sun was low, the moon stood out clearly in the dark afternoon sky, and the question arose: What is there in the nature of man that compels him to walk a lonely beach, to spy on wild creatures, to search to find the undisturbed places beyond?

Incidentally, now that you've come this far east, you ought to continue a couple of blocks farther to the parking area at the absolute end of Route 25, just beyond the New London ferry terminal. If you leave your car there and walk along the beach about one-half mile to the bitter end, you'll enjoy a panorama of Long Island Sound and the Connecticut shore, Block Island Sound, Montauk Point, Gardiners Island, and Gardiners Bay. Directly across the tide rips of Plum Gut is Plum Island, a closed area that is home to the U.S. Department of Agriculture's Animal Disease Center.

47

Montauk Point Parks

This is an extremely popular area, and the crowds may put you off, but don't let them—you'd be missing too much if you did. Choose your time and move away from crowds. Montauk is an experience, and you are apt to enjoy it if you are a loner and nature lover. There's a raw bleakness here: hills of shadbush and bayberry, almost endless dunes, and an incessant surf chewing away at the boulders, tumbling stones that cackle in a noisy babble. We've come here at dawn before the sun was up at least twice and will come again. If you come at this hour, you won't be alone. Surf fishermen will be here before you. You can walk for miles in either direction. We've been here at midday and at sunset, too, lingering afterward in the twilight. So, although it is wiser to rhapsodize about winter, spring, or fall, our experience is that there's something for you in any season at any hour of day in Montauk.

The public lands east of Lake Montauk are quite extensive, as they include the 724-acre state park that extends west from the point about 2 miles to encompass the northern shoreline and Oyster Pond. Directly west of it is the 1,200-acre Suffolk County park that covers Shagwong Point and most of the remaining land east of East Lake Drive (excluding a residential area at the middle section of that road). The last property is the undeveloped 700-acre Camp Hero State Park. It is located south of the highway and away from the lighthouse and formerly was

MONTAUK POINT
PARKS

Lighthouse

Camp Hero
State Park

ATLANTIC
OCEAN

Montauk
Point
State
Park

BLOCK
ISLAND
SOUND

OYSTER
POND

Shagwong
Point

Montauk Point I State Parkway

Hq.

Montauk County Park

30

27

2

BIG
REED
POND

East Lake Drive

LAKE
MONTAUK

1

Airport

0

West Lake Drive

Miles

the site of an Air Force radar station. Although it is not easily accessible, the bluffs are impressive when viewed from the beach.

The present county park headquarters building, called the Third House, dates in part to 1806, when it was erected for those tending cattle on the surrounding 10,000-acre common pasture. Since then it has served as a residence for Theodore Roosevelt and his Rough Riders after the Spanish-American War, and in the 1930s it became the Deep Hollow Guest and Cattle Ranch. Today the only remaining horsey aspect is a riding stable. The hilly terrain here offers good protection from bad weather and thus many varieties of birds and animals inhabit the area.

Where to go at the point? As you leave the state parking area, follow the path north of the lighthouse down into the gully to the little pond. Wildflowers, birds of the thicket, and pond life are here. Then cross over the dunes on to the beach and walk south to the point. If you're here at low tide, you can walk as far south and west along the rocky shore as you are able. The other direction northwest along the beach fronting Block Island Sound is a less crowded walk; the farther you go, the fewer the people and the more abundant the shorebirds. Montauk is a birding area; come equipped with field glasses.

These parks cover a large area, so if you walk only those beaches easily accessible from the main parking area, you have not done justice in exploring the region. If you drive north off the highway on East Lake Drive, stop to sample the county park nature trail, and continue on beyond the lake and the airport to your right to one of the parking places at the very end of the road. From here you can walk eastward on the shore toward Shagwong Point and beyond.

A map of the Montauk area with the various trails is available at the county park headquarters on Route 27. An even more complete map is available from the town of East Hampton; refer to Walk 26 for the address.

If you have questions, call 668–2461 for the state park, and 852–7878 for the Suffolk County park. Both are open daily from 8:00 A.M. to 5:00 P.M

North Shore Beaches and Bluffs

While similar in extent to the marvelous strands of the South Shore, these beaches are quite different in character. They tend in general to be more pebbly, since the sea is constantly eroding, not a long sandbar, but the back side of a glacial moraine. As a result the beaches have lots of stones, from golf ball size up to impressive glacial erratics, so sandy spots for swimming and sunning are somewhat scarce. The stones in turn have been mined from a nearly continuous line of bluffs that line the coast. These can be well over 100 feet high, as at Mt. Sinai, and they are usually wooded up to the edge except where homes have been built. Both these factors often make beach access difficult even while providing fine views out over Long Island Sound. In many places the bluffs are so high and steep that the only way homeowners can get down to the water's edge is by erecting long wooden stairways down the face. They look most impressive when seen from a boat offshore; they must be intimidating close up!

There are a few places in the long stretch east of Port Jefferson where the bluffs are minimal. Most of these spots have either a public or private road down to the beach, for swimmers in the summer and surf fishermen at any time. In general we've usually encountered fewer people on these North Shore beaches than on the south. The parking situation noted for the Atlantic beaches, however, can also apply here.

One other factor that sets these shores apart is the tidal range. On the South Shore the range is only about 3 feet, and between high and low tides the look of the sandy strand changes very little. On the North Shore the range varies from about 4 feet at Horton Point to over 7 feet at Glen Cove. This makes for a markedly different seashore, due to the exposed rocky intertidal zone.

LONG ISLAND SOUND

Bathing Beach

Refreshment Stand

Refreshment Stand Boardwalk

Bathhouse

Play Area

2

1

3

Refreshment Stand

W

W

Play Area

4

Refreshment Stand and Comfort Station

Picnic Area

Maintenance Building

Entrance to Golf Courses

St. Johnland Road

Bridle Path

Tolls

Picnic Area

Parking No. 5

Kings Park

25A

N

SUNKEN MEADOW STATE PARK

0   ¼   ½

Miles

48

Sunken Meadow
State Park

Sunken Meadow State Park is a grand place for walking, most
particularly when it's not swimming weather. Take a nice, crisp
fall weekend to go or a soft spring day or even a misty summer's
day, for there are miles to explore, with an interesting inlet to
the east, a bridle path to the south, the beach itself as far west
as you could wish, and in the middle of it all a fine .75-mile
boardwalk.

This beautiful park, which has one of the best sand beaches
on the North Shore, was opened to the public back in the 1920s
when the legendary Robert Moses acquired an abandoned estate
here. He saw its possibilities for a public recreation area on the
sound directly north of the state park that bears his name on the
South Shore. Now there are four large parking lots, three golf
courses, picnic areas and playgrounds, and refreshment stands.
Sunken Meadow is a highly organized place, well adapted to lots
of visitors, but it all quiets down in the off-season.

The walk we enjoy the most is to take the Greenbelt Trail
east, from its beginning at the footbridge close to the southwest
end of parking field 3, along the high bluffs to Old Dock Road.
There you can drop down to beach level and return along the
shore until you can cross over again to gain lot 3. This 2.5-mile
loop gives you fine views of the Nissequogue inlet and estuary,

salt meadows, and a long stretch of beach extending in both directions. If field 3 is closed, park in field 1 and walk east to the bridge.

As you might expect, the 200 acres of sandy bluffs, brackish creeks, salt marshes, and heavily wooded uplands offer excellent habitat for birds in all seasons. 84 varieties are common in one season or another, and sixty more are occasionally seen here, so bring your binoculars.

The park is open 6:30 A.M. to sunset in the summer season, with a $4.00 toll (but free before 8:00 A.M. and after 4:00 P.M). The rest of the year hours are 7:00 A.M. to sunset, with no toll. Questions? Call 269–4333.

The best roads to take to reach the park are major arteries such as the Long Island Expressway (Route 495), Jericho Turnpike (Route 25), Northern State Parkway, and Route 25A. All of them intersect with the sole entrance road, the Sunken Meadow Parkway.

49

Nissequogue Estuary

A blazed trail, the Long Island Greenbelt, winds across the full width of Long Island and has since 1978, going northward 34 miles from Great South Bay to Long Island Sound. This was made possible through the inspiration and initiative of the Long Island Greenbelt Trail Conference, combined with the cooperative effort of the towns of Islip and Smithtown, Suffolk County and New York State, and the financial support of a dozen public-spirited, ecology-minded corporations with a stake in Long Island's future. It is a noteworthy accomplishment.

Anyone may walk the trail, which has locked gates where it enters nature preserves, but you must have a permit to get the lock combinations (call 265–1054, Caleb Smith State Park). The Conference prints a map guide with nine maps that show clearly the route the trail follows, and this is obtainable through the Long Island Greenbelt Trail Conference, Inc., 23 Deer Path Road, Central Islip, NY 11722; 360–0753.

After leaving Blydenburgh County Park and Caleb Smith State Park, both of which have walks (33 and 21) that can conveniently be done from a central location, the Greenbelt Trail heads north toward its end at Sunken Meadow State Park. This section is a linear one, with more road walking than is desireable, so we can't really recommend the first part of it.

Most of the last 4 miles, however, are so rewarding that we urge you to find a friend and spot cars at each end so you can

NISSEQUOGUE ESTUARY

N

LONG ISLAND SOUND

Landing Road

Riviera Road

Rose Street

W

W

W

W

P

St. Johnland Road

Kings Park State Hospital

Obadiah Smith House

HARRISON POND

SAN REMO

25A

Old Dock Rd.

Sunken Meadow State Park

KINGS PARK

Sunken Meadow Parkway

Miles

0   1   2

cover it more easily. The trail basically follows the south shore of the Nissequogue River, sometimes close to the water, sometimes well above it on bluffs.

To start at the south end of this lovely stretch, find the corner where Route 25A makes a right-angle turn in San Remo, about 1.7 miles north of the junction with Route 25 in Smithtown. At the corner go straight east on Rose Street for about 0.4 mile until it ends at Landing Avenue. Turn left there, and in 0.2 mile turn right into the long downhill driveway of the Smithtown Landing Club Town Park. Go down to the end, park there amid the golfers, and find the Greenbelt blazes. They are vertical white blazes about 2 inches by 4 inches painted on trees, rocks, and posts and should be easy to pick up here. The trail heads north along the shoreline again, reaches Riviera Road, and continues on it along the curve of the river. When you reach St. Johnland Road, the trail goes right for a short distance. Right across the street the parking area for the Harrison Pond Town Park is an alternate place to leave a car.

Just below the Obadiah Smith House, the trail leaves the road and cuts north across the marsh. Go in here at the double blaze. Remember that a single blaze means you're still on the right track; a double one signals a change in direction.

The path crosses through tall reeds, follows along the river, climbs a bluff for a fine view, and continues on to Old Dock Road. Here there are a restaurant and boating facilities and another place you can park off-season.

When you take the trail up the 150-foot bluff to the west, you enter Sunken Meadow State Park and can now follow the route along the top until you come down into the developed part of the park. There the trail makes a sharp turn across a footbridge to end just across the road from parking lot 3.

From this last stretch of bluffs, you can see where the river reaches the sound; beyond it is Short Beach, which belongs to the village of Nissequogue, and Crane Neck Point across Smithtown Bay. Across the sound is Connecticut, of course, and the city with the tall buildings is Bridgeport. There are always boats of many sizes, which move in a businesslike way across the sound's waters and, in the river, swans, which have a close affinity to Long Island. This section of the trail provides picture postcard views all along the bluffs, and when the waterfowl migrate, it can be spectacular. The bluffs are popular, so for the quiet moods that the trail does have, it is best to walk here early in the morning—or late on a summer's day to watch the sunset.

50

Wildwood State Park

Wildwood State Park is well out on the island, 73 miles east of New York City. It is roughly rectangular and has a frontage of about 1.5 miles on the Long Island Sound. Situated on high ground with high bluffs, it covers just over 500 acres. There is good walking along the pebbly North Shore beach here. Also, within the park, there are about 5 miles of trails through woodland areas all amply cleared and easy walking straightaway, fairly level, nothing strenuous. It is a place that is open, protected, quiet, wooded. And you can walk at a good clip.

Many of the North Shore beaches are private, not allowing easy access without trespassing, but there is a large parking lot with a broad walkway leading down a gradual slope less than a half mile to the beach. The sand doesn't shift along these North Shore beaches as rapidly as it does along the Atlantic. The water freezes up much more quickly and warms earlier in the spring. The ground is gravelly, and there are quite a few boulders, debris of the glacial period. Protected as the beach is by these high bluffs, it is a marked contrast to the ocean shore and offers good variety to a beach walker. There's less severe buffeting in windy weather, too. Those close relatives of the crab, barnacles, have attached themselves to all boulders. Seaweed in many forms is exposed. Periwinkles and whelks abound. The narrow strip of this tidal zone teems with life, hidden between rocks and usually

WILDWOOD STATE PARK

N

LONG ISLAND SOUND

Sound Avenue

Bathhouse

Camping

Hulse Landing Road

54

Park
Entrance

1

½

0

Miles

ignored by all except the most curious persons. Wildwood State Park, however, does have a considerable population because of a large tent camping area and trailer camp, so it is a popular weekend retreat and no place to walk the beach during summer months if you seek a lonely stretch. Plan to walk in Wildwood out of season, when it will be rewarding. It's open all year, dawn to dusk.

To get to Wildwood, take Route 54, Hulse Landing Road, north from Route 25A. It is just east of Wading River (929–4314).

Quite naturally the inland trails are places less frequented, although they are more protected and easier walking, but do also enjoy the views from the trail along the west bluff. If it weren't for the trees along the North Shore, erosion would have taken most of Long Island into the sound. So walk here to discover the woodland, the home of numerous insects, birds, and mammals, and bring along a curiosity to get to know still another tree, shrub, or creature with whom we share the earth.

REEVES BEACH

LONG ISLAND SOUND

N

Roanoke Point

Ship Hulks

Friars Head

Roanoke Avenue

Reeves Park

Park Road

Horton Avenue

Osborn

Sound Avenue

0   ½   1
Miles

51

Reeves Beach

The town of Riverhead maintains a beach at the end of Roanoke Avenue on Long Island Sound. Off-season, there is usually no problem parking, though during summer months a permit is required (obtainable at the town recreation department). The bluffs on the sound are extremely high, the beach at the tide line quite pebbly with some impressive glacial erratics, and, just west a half mile, strewn with two ship hulks, wrecks of some time past. It's a steep walk down to the beach from the parking spot. Turn left and walk a couple of hundred yards, and you will be alone.

For miles along here the border of high wooded bluffs obscures any houses, and there is a feeling of immense loneliness. There are especially wide areas and big tangles of the purple beach pea, sea rocket, and bishop's weed. Some reeds at the base of the bluffs are so tall you can be completely concealed by them. It is nice exploring territory. Tangles of growth conceal old driftwood, and there are wild beach flowers. Fishing offshore here must be pretty good; there are frequently clusters of small boats bobbing not far out and an occasional surfcaster.

We have walked this beach many times, but never during swimming season. Its setting—the beach is tucked down under a high ridge—appeals to us. In a winter rain the Connecticut shoreline is completely obscured. With snow on the frozen ground, you cover distances faster. In early spring we find trailing arbutus on paths up the bluffs, with wintergreen and partridge berry. The trailing arbutus is particularly satisfying to come upon in blossom, such a delicate fragrance and the tiny, palest lavender petals. On fresh, bright sunny weekends, the promise of a good breeze brings many sails out on the sound, and the clarity lets you see details on the opposite shores. Falling autumn leaves pile up in the gullies, cover paths, and rustle when you pass along. Because we never have any particular objective in mind, we always look at a watch as we start off headed west, and when we remember to look again, we are always surprised by the lateness of the hour. We usually take along field glasses and a camera.

How to get there? Follow Roanoke Avenue north from the Route 58 traffic circle in Riverhead until it ends at Sound Avenue. Then turn left, west, and go a short distance to the second road, Park Road. Turn right, north, and follow up and down a hill or two. The road ends in a nice, new parking area that overlooks Reeves Beach.

52

Horton Point Beach

The Horton Point Lighthouse sits serenely, looking something like a canvas by Edward Hopper, high over the waters of Long Island Sound facing Connecticut. It is the chief ornament of a tree-shaded Town of Southold park, which is a beautiful place to picnic. It should be noted that on a visit to Southold as a young surveyor, George Washington recommended that a navigational beacon be set up on this spot. Today it houses an excellent, small marine museum which, like the lighthouse, has been sponsored and improved by the Southold Historical Society.

One hundred thirty-two wooden steps take you down to the boulder-strewn beach. In all kinds of weather it is picturesque because of fisher-folk. They take blackfish from around those rocks. They dig their poles into the sand, light their pipes, and keep an eye on the floats, ready to jump and reel in when they bob. We always check to see if they have a few swimming about in their pails.

Walking on Horton's beach can be rough because of the pebbles, but good for massaging the insteps. Snorkeling is popular here. It's one of the few places on Long Island where we see people in wet suits with scuba tanks and flippers. The huge rocks are relics of the Ice Age.

There is a long beach stretch here to the west that seems uninhabited, very wide with lots of driftwood. And the flotsam that heaves itself up on the beach is fascinating.

Standing on these North Shore bluffs makes Long Island's formation in the geological past become fundamentally clear. You can imagine the great pushing blade of the glaciers, for geologists say Long Island is wholly the result of the glaciers, shoving a wide, wide swath of sand, soil, rock, tops of mountains southward like a massive bulldozer and piling it here. Then the ice melted and the waters ran off, washing the soils southward into a plain. The colossal scale of the whole thing can be appreciated when you realize that the ocean was raised to its present level, more than 300 feet higher than it had been, by the melted ice to form the Long Island Sound. And what capriciousness there was in shoving and raising the level of the waters can be seen in the structure of peninsulas and spits and tiny islands that make up the shape of the map today.

The force that could bring these huge boulders can be better appreciated when you walk along the beach here, comparing your size to their size. Surely the experience is a universal one, and it is one that will linger with you.

The museum alone is worth a visit if you have any interest in matters nautical or, indeed, local. The collection of scrimshaw, tools, maps, letters, ships' logs and journals, paintings, and more is splendid. One can also climb the tower to inspect the working light and enjoy the view. The museum is normally open on weekends from 11:30 A.M. to 4:00 P.M., between Memorial Day and Labor Day, but it would be well to check with the historical society in Southold before your visit (765–5500), as special visits can be arranged at other times.

A word on getting here. Take the Route 25/48 divided highway (North Road) east from Mattituck until you come to the turnoff for Southold Village (Youngs Avenue). Instead of going right, turn left on Youngs and follow it, past the jog at Sound View Avenue, to the very end.

About the Authors

"We are not hikers—we aren't that goal-oriented." So say the Albrights, trying to make the distinction between walking to get somewhere and walking for fun. For them walking is to look and listen to all the sights and sounds of the woods, the meadows, and the sea.

Priscilla and Rod Albright lived in New York most of their adult lives; having come East to college, they stayed right on. Rod was a television producer for a large advertising agency, and Priscilla served on the boards of several social services agencies.

Now retired, they do their daily walks from three different bases: in summer on an island in the Bay of Fundy where the craggy shores offer some scrambling and the woodland paths are full of birds and blueberries; in fall and spring they walk in the foothills of the White Mountains from a cottage in South Parsonsfield, Maine, near the New Hampshire border; come the depths of winter, a small Airstream trailer goes with them to Florida and Florida trails on pine needles or to the Southwest to walk in canyons or the floor of deserts because they are insatiably curious about the natural world.

Robert L. Wendt, who updated and revised the fourth and fifth editions, has been an active walker and outdoorsman in the New York area for many years. Active in the Appalachian Mountain Club and in mapping Long Island trails, he brings broad experience in the field to this task.

Standing on these North Shore bluffs makes Long Island's formation in the geological past become fundamentally clear. You can imagine the great pushing blade of the glaciers, for geologists say Long Island is wholly the result of the glaciers, shoving a wide, wide swath of sand, soil, rock, tops of mountains southward like a massive bulldozer and piling it here. Then the ice melted and the waters ran off, washing the soils southward into a plain. The colossal scale of the whole thing can be appreciated when you realize that the ocean was raised to its present level, more than 300 feet higher than it had been, by the melted ice to form the Long Island Sound. And what capriciousness there was in shoving and raising the level of the waters can be seen in the structure of peninsulas and spits and tiny islands that make up the shape of the map today.

The force that could bring these huge boulders can be better appreciated when you walk along the beach here, comparing your size to their size. Surely the experience is a universal one, and it is one that will linger with you.

The museum alone is worth a visit if you have any interest in matters nautical or, indeed, local. The collection of scrimshaw, tools, maps, letters, ships' logs and journals, paintings, and more is splendid. One can also climb the tower to inspect the working light and enjoy the view. The museum is normally open on weekends from 11:30 A.M. to 4:00 P.M., between Memorial Day and Labor Day, but it would be well to check with the historical society in Southold before your visit (765–5500), as special visits can be arranged at other times.

A word on getting here. Take the Route 25/48 divided highway (North Road) east from Mattituck until you come to the turnoff for Southold Village (Youngs Avenue). Instead of going right, turn left on Youngs and follow it, past the jog at Sound View Avenue, to the very end.

About the Authors

"We are not hikers—we aren't that goal-oriented." So say the Albrights, trying to make the distinction between walking to get somewhere and walking for fun. For them walking is to look and listen to all the sights and sounds of the woods, the meadows, and the sea.

Priscilla and Rod Albright lived in New York most of their adult lives; having come East to college, they stayed right on. Rod was a television producer for a large advertising agency, and Priscilla served on the boards of several social services agencies.

Now retired, they do their daily walks from three different bases: in summer on an island in the Bay of Fundy where the craggy shores offer some scrambling and the woodland paths are full of birds and blueberries; in fall and spring they walk in the foothills of the White Mountains from a cottage in South Parsonsfield, Maine, near the New Hampshire border; come the depths of winter, a small Airstream trailer goes with them to Florida and Florida trails on pine needles or to the Southwest to walk in canyons or the floor of deserts because they are insatiably curious about the natural world.

Robert L. Wendt, who updated and revised the fourth and fifth editions, has been an active walker and outdoorsman in the New York area for many years. Active in the Appalachian Mountain Club and in mapping Long Island trails, he brings broad experience in the field to this task.

Here's what kids have to say to
Mary Pope Osborne, author of
the Magic Tree House series:

Your books have gotten me interested in reading. That has made my parents very happy.—Philip J.

I wish I could keep all your books in a glass case with a golden key.—Luke R.

I love your Magic Tree House series. I even pretend that I am Jack.—Tommy C.

I'd like to be a writer just like you.—Meghan G.

Your books really make me dream.—Kurt K.

I think you are the best writer in all mankind!—Heather O.

Write to Mary Pope Osborne yourself!

Magic Tree House #8

Midnight on the Moon

by Mary Pope Osborne

illustrated by Sal Murdocca

Scholastic Inc.

New York Toronto London Auckland Sydney

For Jacob and Elena Levi
and Aram and Molly Hanessian

ISBN 0-590-98825-5

Text copyright © 1996 by Mary Pope Osborne.
Illustrations copyright © 1996 by Sal Murdocca.
All rights reserved. Published by Scholastic Inc.,
555 Broadway, New York, NY 10012, by arrangement with
Random House, Inc.

24 23 22 21 20 19 18 17 16 15   1 2 3 4 5/0

Printed in the U.S.A.   40

First Scholastic printing, January 1997

Contents

Prologue

One summer day in Frog Creek, Pennsylvania, a mysterious tree house appeared in the woods.

Eight-year-old Jack and his seven-year-old sister, Annie, climbed into the tree house.

The tree house was filled with books and it was *magic*. It could go any place that was in a book. All Jack and Annie had to do was to point to a picture and wish to go there.

They visited dinosaurs, knights, an Egyptian queen, pirates, ninjas, and the Amazon rain forest.

Along the way, they discovered that the tree house belonged to Morgan le Fay. Morgan was a magical librarian from the time of King Arthur. She traveled through time and space, gathering books for her library.

One day, Jack and Annie found a note that said Morgan was under a spell. Jack and Annie set out in the magic tree house to find four special things that would free her.

With the help of a mouse named Peanut, Jack and Annie found the first thing in old Japan, the second in the Amazon rain forest, and the third in the Ice Age.

Now Jack, Annie, and Peanut are ready to find the last thing...in *Midnight on the Moon*.

1

By Moonlight

"Jack!" whispered a voice.

Jack opened his eyes. He saw a figure in the moonlight.

"Wake up. Get dressed." It was his sister, Annie.

Jack turned on his lamp. He rubbed his eyes.

Annie was standing beside his bed. She wore jeans and a sweatshirt.

"Let's go to the tree house," she said.

"What time is it?" asked Jack. He put on his glasses.

"Don't look at your clock," said Annie.

Jack looked at his clock. "Oh, man," he said. "It's midnight. It's too dark."

"No, it isn't. The moon makes it bright enough to see," said Annie.

"Wait till morning," said Jack.

"No—now," said Annie. "We have to find the fourth M thing. I have a feeling that the full moon might help us."

"That's nuts," said Jack. "I want to sleep."

"You can sleep when we come back home," said Annie. "No time will have passed."

Jack sighed. "Oh, brother," he said.

But he got out of bed.

"Yay!" whispered Annie. "Meet you at the back door." She tiptoed out of Jack's room.

Jack yawned. He pulled on his jeans and sneakers and a sweatshirt. He put his notebook and pencil into his backpack. Then he crept down the stairs.

Annie opened the back door. Quietly, they stepped outside.

"Wait—" said Jack. "We need a flashlight."

"No, we don't. I told you—the moon will light our way," said Annie. And she took off.

Jack sighed, then followed her.

Annie was right, thought Jack. The moon was so bright that he could see his shadow. Everything seemed washed with silver.

Soon they left their street. Annie led the way into the Frog Creek woods. It was much darker under the shadows of the trees.

Jack looked up, searching for the tree house.

"There!" said Annie.

The magic tree house was shining in the moonlight.

Annie grabbed the rope ladder and started climbing up.

"Careful—go slowly," said Jack.

He followed her up the ladder and into the tree house.

Moonlight streamed through the window.

It shone on the letter M that shimmered on the wooden floor.

It shone on the three M things that rested on the M: a *moonstone* from the time of the ninjas, a *mango* from the Amazon rain forest, and a *mammoth bone* from the Ice Age.

"We need just one more M thing," said Annie, "to free Morgan from her spell."

Squeak.

"Peanut!" said Annie.

In the dim light, Jack saw a tiny mouse. She sat on an open book.

"You didn't expect to see us this late, did you?" said Annie.

She picked up Peanut. And Jack picked up the open book.

"So where are we going this time?" Annie asked him.

Jack held the book up to the moonlight.

"Uh-oh," he said. "I knew we should have brought a flashlight. I can't read a thing."

He could make out diagrams and shadowy pictures. But he couldn't read a word.

"Look at the cover," said Annie.

The letters were bigger on the cover. Jack squinted at them.

"It's called *Hello, Moon*," he said.

Annie gasped. "We're going to the moon?"

"Of course not," said Jack. "It's impossible to go to the moon without tons of equipment."

"Why?"

"There's no air. We couldn't breathe. Not only that, we'd boil to death if it was day and freeze to death if it was night."

"Yikes," said Annie. "So where do you think we are going?"

"Maybe a place where people train to be astronauts," said Jack.

"That sounds neat," said Annie.

"Yeah," said Jack. He'd always wanted to meet astronauts and space scientists.

"So say the wish," said Annie.

Jack opened the book again. He pointed to a picture of a dome-shaped structure.

"I wish we could go there," he said.

9

The wind started to blow.

The tree house started to spin.

It spun faster and faster and faster.

Then everything was silent.

Absolutely silent. As quiet and still as silence could be.

2

Space Motel

Jack opened his eyes.

He looked out the window. The tree house had landed inside a large white room.

"What kind of training place is this?" asked Annie.

"I don't know," said Jack.

The room was round. It had no windows. It had white floors and a curved wall lit by bright lights.

"Hello!" Annie called.

There was no answer.

Where were all the astronauts and space scientists? Jack wondered.

"There's nobody here," said Annie.

"How do you know?" said Jack.

"I just feel it," said Annie.

"We'd better find out where we are," said Jack.

He looked at the page in the moon book. He read the words below the picture of the dome.

> A moon base was built on the moon in the year 2031. The top of the dome slides open to let spacecrafts enter and leave.

"Oh, man—" Jack whispered.

"What's wrong?" said Annie.

Jack's heart pounded with excitement. He could hardly speak. "We've landed inside a moon base," he said.

"So...?" said Annie.

"So the moon base is on the moon!" said Jack.

Annie's eyes widened. "We're *on* the moon?" she asked.

Jack nodded. "The book says the moon base was built in the year 2031," he said. "So this book was written *after* that! Which means this book is from the *future!*"

"Oh, wow," said Annie. "Morgan must have gone forward in time to borrow it from a future library."

"Right," said Jack. "And now we're in the future, on the moon."

Squeak, squeak!

Annie and Jack looked at Peanut. The mouse was running around in circles.

"Poor Peanut," said Annie.

She tried to pick the mouse up. But Peanut hid behind the mango on the letter M.

"Maybe she's nervous about being on the moon," said Annie.

"She's not the only one," said Jack. He let out a deep breath, then he pushed his glasses into place.

"So what's a moon base?" asked Annie.

Jack looked at the book. He read aloud:

When scientists visit the moon for short periods, they eat and sleep in the moon base.

"A space motel!" said Annie.

"I guess," said Jack. He read more:

The small base has a landing chamber
and a room for storing spacesuits.
Air and temperature controls make
breathing possible.

"So that's why we can breathe," Jack said.

"Let's explore," said Annie. "We have to
find the fourth thing for Morgan."

"No, first we should study this map," said
Jack. He pulled out his notebook.

"*You* study it," said Annie.

Jack copied the map. Then he drew in the
tree house.

"Okay," he said. He pointed at the X in his drawing. "We're *here*."

Jack looked up. Annie was gone.

"Oh, brother," Jack said. As usual, she had left without him. Before they could even make a plan.

Jack put the moon book and pencil into his pack. Carrying his notebook and backpack, he started out the window.

Squeak! Squeak!

Jack looked back at Peanut. The mouse was running back and forth on the M.

"Stay here and be safe," said Jack. "We'll be back soon."

Jack swung himself over the window sill. His feet touched the floor of the landing chamber.

"Annie!" he called.

There was no answer.

Jack looked at his diagram.

It showed only one way to go. Jack walked along the curved white wall to the stairs.

He climbed the steps to a hallway.

"Jack—hurry!" Annie was at the end of the hallway, standing in the airlock. She peered out a window in a giant door.

Jack hurried toward her. Annie stepped aside so he could look out the window, too.

"Oh, man," said Jack. What he saw took his breath away.

He stared at a rocky gray land. The land was filled with giant craters and tall mountains. The sun was shining. But the sky was ink-black!

"Say hi to the moon," Annie said softly.

3

Open Sesame!

"The fourth M thing must be out there," said Annie.

Beside the door was a button with the word OPEN on it. Annie reached for the button.

"Wait!" Jack grabbed her hand. "There's no air on the moon. Remember?"

"Oh. Right. But we have to go out to find the M thing."

"Let's see what the book says," said Jack.

He pulled the book out of his pack. He flipped through it until he found a page that showed the surface of the moon. He read aloud:

> It takes fourteen Earth days to equal
> one day on the moon. No air protects
> the moon from the sun's rays, so
> daytime heat reaches 260 degrees.

Jack looked at Annie. "I told you our blood would boil if we went out there," he said.

"Yuck," she said.

Jack read from the book again:

> Moon scientists wear spacesuits,
> which have controls to keep them
> from getting too hot or too cold. They
> have tanks, which provide air for two
> hours.

"Where do we get spacesuits?" asked Annie. She looked around then trotted back down the hall. "Maybe there...?"

Jack was studying his map. "Let's try the spacesuit storeroom."

"Don't look at the map," said Annie. "Look at the *real* room!"

Jack glanced up. Annie was peering through a doorway off the hall.

"There's a ton of space stuff in here!" she said.

Jack went to look.

Bulky white suits hung from hangers. Air tanks, helmets, gloves, and boots sat in neat rows on shelves.

"Wow, it's like the armor room in a castle," said Jack.

"Yeah, with huge armor," said Annie.

"Let's pick out the smallest stuff," said Jack, "The suits can go over our clothes."

Annie found the smallest white suit. And Jack found the next smallest. They stepped into them.

Then Annie locked Jack's air tank into place.

"Thanks," he said. And he did the same for her.

"Thanks," she said.

"Gloves?" said Jack. He and Annie pulled on white gloves.

"Boots?" said Annie. They each pulled on a pair of huge white boots.

"Helmets?" said Jack. He reached for a helmet.

"Wow, they're pretty light," he said. "I thought they'd be like knights' helmets."

Jack and Annie put the helmets on. They locked each other's into place.

"I can't move my head right or left," said Annie.

"Me neither," said Jack. "Let's try walking."

Jack and Annie moved clumsily around the room. Jack felt like a fat snowman.

"Close your visor," said Annie.

They both closed their see-through visors. Cool air filled Jack's helmet.

"I CAN BREATHE!" Annie yelled. Her voice boomed in Jack's ears.

"Ow! Talk quietly," Jack said. "We have two-way radios inside our helmets."

"Sorry," whispered Annie.

Jack put the moon book back in his pack. Then he slung the pack over his shoulder.

"Okay!" he said. "Remember, we only have two hours of air in our tanks. So we need to find the fourth M thing really fast."

"I hope we can find it," said Annie.

"Me too," said Jack. He knew they could not go home until they did.

"Let's go," said Annie. She gave Jack a little push.

"Watch it. No goofing off," he said. "We don't want to fall over in these suits."

"Just go—go!" said Annie. She pushed him out of the room. They walked back to the airlock.

"Ready?" said Annie. "Open sesame!" She pressed the OPEN button. A door slowly slid closed behind them. A door opened in front of them.

And Jack and Annie stepped out onto the moon.

4

Moon Rabbits

"Oh, wow!" said Annie. She took a step forward.

But Jack stood frozen. He wanted to get a good look at everything first.

He stared at the ground. He was standing in a layer of gray dust as fine as powder.

Footprints were everywhere. Jack wondered who had made them.

He reached into his pack for the moon book. To his surprise, it was as light as a feather!

He found a picture of footprints on the moon. He read:

> The moon has no rain or wind to blow
> the dust around. So footprints will
> never wear away naturally, not even in
> a billion years.

"Oh, man," Jack said.

The moon was the stillest place he had ever, *ever* been. It was as still as a picture. And its stillness would never, ever end.

Jack stared at the ink-black sky. A lovely blue-and-white ball glowed far away.

Earth.

For the first time, it really hit Jack. They were in outer space.

"Look!" Annie cried, laughing.

She bounded past Jack—almost flying

through the air. She landed on her feet. Then she jumped again.

"I'm a moon rabbit," she called.

Jack laughed. How does she do that? he wondered. He turned a page and read:

> A person weighs less on the moon
> because of the moon's low gravity and
> lack of air. If you weigh 60 pounds on
> Earth, you would only weigh 10
> pounds on the moon.

"Don't just stand there reading!" said Annie, grabbing the book from Jack's gloved hand. She tossed it into space.

It flew far away.

Jack started after it.

He bounded up and down. *Boing! Boing! Boing!* Now *he* felt as light as a feather.

"Look!" he called to Annie. "I'm a moon rabbit, too."

Where Jack's boots hit the ground, moon-dust gracefully sprayed into space.

The book had landed at the edge of a shallow crater.

When Jack reached it, he tried to stop. But his feet slipped.

He fell right over and lay on his side. He tried to stand. But he was off-balance.

He tried again. But the dust was just too deep. And his spacesuit was too clumsy.

"You okay?" asked Annie.

"I can't get up," said Jack.

"You shouldn't have been goofing off," said Annie wisely.

"You goofed off first," said Jack. "Now, help me up, please."

Annie started toward him.

"Don't fall, too," warned Jack.

"I won't." Annie moved very slowly. She half floated, half walked.

"Give me your hand," she said.

Annie grabbed Jack's hand. She pressed her boot against his and pulled him up.

"Thanks," he said.

"No problem," she said. "It was easy. You were really light."

"Thank goodness," said Jack. "It's impossible to get up alone."

He picked up the moon book. It was covered with dust. He brushed it off.

"Oh, wow! Look!" said Annie. She stood at the edge of the crater.

"What is it?" said Jack.

"A moon buggy!" said Annie.

The buggy was parked in the crater. It had four huge wheels.

"Let's go for a ride," said Annie.

"We can't," said Jack. "We just have two hours of air in our tanks. Remember?"

"I bet we'll find the M thing faster if we take the moon buggy!" Annie bounded into the crater.

"But we can't drive!" said Jack.

"I bet I can drive *this*," said Annie. "It looks easy. Come on!"

She jumped into the driver's seat.

"But you don't have a license!" said Jack.

"Who cares?" said Annie. "There aren't any roads on the moon, or stoplights, or policemen either."

She was right, Jack thought.

"Well, go slow," he said. And he climbed in beside her.

Annie pushed a button labeled ON.

The moon buggy lurched backward.

"Yikes!" said Annie.

"Step on the brake!" said Jack.

Annie pressed a pedal on the floor. The buggy stopped with a jerk.

"Whew," she said.

"It must be in reverse," said Jack. "Let me study this—"

But before he could study anything, Annie pushed another button.

The buggy tilted back. Its front wheels started to rise into the air.

"Let me out of here!" said Jack.

Annie pushed more buttons.

The buggy's front wheels landed back on the ground. And the buggy leaped forward.

"*Slower!*" said Jack.

"I can't," said Annie. "I don't know how!"

Annie steered the buggy over the tracks on the ground. The wide wheels kept it from sinking into the deep dust.

"Careful!" said Jack.

The buggy zoomed out of the crater.

Gray clouds of dust rose behind them as they took off across the moon.

5

Hang On!

Annie drove the moon buggy over bumps and hollows. It bucked like a bronco.

"I'm going through *there*!" She pointed to an opening between two mountains.

Jack held on to the dashboard.

The buggy bumped toward the opening and shot through.

On the other side, the ground was even rockier.

"Look for the fo-fourth M thing!" said Annie, bouncing up and down.

Jack groaned. Looking for anything on this wild ride was impossible.

"Sl-slow d-down!" he said.

"How?"

"Try pressing on the b-brake pedal. On the f-floor—slowly!"

Annie pressed on the brake.

The buggy slowed down. Jack sighed with

relief. The ride was still bumpy. But now, at least, he could take a good look at the moon.

He had never been to such a colorless, barren place. There was no green, no blue, no red.

No water, no trees, no clouds.

Only giant gray rocks and craters—*and an American flag.*

"Oh, man," said Jack. "That's from the first astronauts who landed on the moon!"

"And look—a telescope!" said Annie.

She drove near the flag and telescope. Then she put her foot on the brake until the buggy stopped.

She pressed a button that said OFF. Then she and Jack hopped out.

They took slow giant steps to the site of the first moon landing.

Beside the flag was a sign. Annie read it aloud:

HERE MEN FROM THE PLANET EARTH
FIRST SET FOOT UPON THE MOON,
JULY 1969 A.D.
WE CAME IN PEACE
FOR ALL MANKIND.

"That's a good message," said Jack.

He handed the moon book to Annie. Then he took out his notebook and pencil to copy the sign.

"Let's leave our own message," said Annie.

"What should we say?" said Jack.

"The same thing," said Annie. "But say we are the first kids."

Jack turned to a new page in his notebook. In big letters he wrote their message.

"Now we have to sign it," Annie said.

Jack signed his name.

Then he passed the notebook and pencil to Annie. She signed her name and passed the notebook back.

Jack tore out the piece of paper. He put it by the flag.

Today the first kids from the planet
Earth came to the Moon. We came in
peace for all children.
                    Jack
                ANNIE

No wind would ever blow the message
away. No rain would ever fall on it.

It would be there forever, unless someone
moved it.

Thinking of "forever" made Jack feel
dizzy. He shook his head to clear his thoughts.
Then he remembered the time. Had two
hours passed yet?

"I wish I had a watch," he said, standing
up. "We might be running out of time."

"Oh, wow. A moon man!" said Annie.

"What?" Jack turned to look at her.

She was staring through the telescope.

Jack walked over to the telescope. Annie stepped aside so he could look, too.

Jack gasped. In the distance, something was flying above the ground.

It looked like a giant man in a spacesuit.

6

High Jump

"Who is *that?*" said Jack.

"I don't know," said Annie. "But we'll soon find out!" She started waving.

"No!" said Jack. He grabbed her arm. "Let's go back to the base—before he gets here!"

"Why?" said Annie.

"We don't know who he is!" said Jack. "We don't know if he's friendly or mean or what."

"But we can't go back," said Annie. "We haven't found the fourth M thing yet.

We won't be able to go home."

"It doesn't matter. We can lock the door at the moon base until he goes away," said Jack. "Then we can get new air tanks!"

Jack hurried to the moon buggy. "Come on!" He jumped into the driver's seat.

Annie gave a little wave to the dot in the sky. Then she climbed into the moon buggy.

The buggy took off.

"Careful!" said Annie.

They bumped over the rocks as Jack turned the buggy around. Then they zoomed toward the pass.

Jack steered around craters and rocks. More than once the buggy nearly tipped over.

"Whoa! Slow down!" said Annie.

They were almost at the mountain pass. Suddenly, a cloud of dust flew up in front of them. The ground trembled.

"Watch it!" cried Annie.

Jack couldn't see a thing.

He stepped on the brake. The buggy jerked to a stop.

The dust settled.

A giant rock had fallen into the narrow pass. It was stuck between two walls of rock. They were trapped!

Jack quickly found a picture of a giant rock in the moon book. He read aloud:

> Rocks of all sizes crash into the moon
> from outer space. These rocks are
> called meteorites.

"We're lucky that meteorite didn't land on *us*," said Jack.

"Yeah, and I guess it's too big to be the M thing," said Annie. She had climbed out of the moon buggy and was standing by the meteorite.

It was more than twice as tall as she was.

Jack looked at the black sky. The flying thing was nowhere in sight—yet.

"We'll have to jump over it," Annie said.

"Jump? I don't think so," said Jack. "It's too high."

"I'm going to try anyway," said Annie.

"Wait. Let's think first," said Jack.

But Annie was already backing up.

"One, two, three—go!" she shouted, and took giant, leaping steps toward the meteorite.

When Annie got close to the rock, she pushed off the ground. Then she flew through space and disappeared behind the meteorite.

"Annie!" Jack called.

There was no answer.

"Oh, brother," Jack said. He backed up and took off toward the rock. He jumped as high as he could. Then he was flying through space.

Jack hit the ground and fell facedown into the the dust.

Jack tried to stand. But his suit was too bulky. He tried to roll over. But his suit made even that impossible.

"Oh, no," he groaned. "Not again."

"Are you here?" asked Annie. "Did you make it?"

"Yes!" Jack was relieved to hear her voice. But he couldn't turn his head to see her. He could only hear her over the radio.

Can you help me up?" he asked.

"Nope," said Annie

"Why not?"

"I fell down, too," she said.

44

"Oh, brother," Jack sighed. "Now we are *really* in trouble."

He tried to stand again. And failed.

"Can you see anything?" he asked.

"Just the sky," said Annie. "Wow, is it weird…"

"I'm worried about our air tanks," said Jack. "I feel like it's been two hours."

"Ja-ack…" said Annie.

"And what about that moon man?" said Jack. "Where did he go to?"

"Jack!" whispered Annie.

"What?"

"He's here," she said. "The moon man is here."

"*What?*"

"He's standing above me."

7

The Moon Man

Jack's heart nearly stopped.

He could hear Annie talking.

"Hi," she said. "We come in peace."

There was silence. Then Jack heard Annie say, "Thank you. I have to help my brother up now."

A moment later, Annie rolled Jack onto his back.

She grabbed his hand and pulled him up.

"Thanks," said Jack, once he was standing.

The moon man was a few feet away. His

face was hidden by a metal visor.

He looked like a spaceman. A *huge* space-man—with a giant tank on his back. It was as big as a refrigerator.

"That's a jet pack!" said Jack. "I've seen pictures of future astronauts flying with those things. It's like a mini-spaceship. Right?"

The moon man didn't answer.

"I don't think he can hear us," said Annie. "He's not hooked up to our radio."

"Oh, right," said Jack. "I'll write him a message!"

"Good idea," said Annie.

Jack pulled out his notebook and pencil. He wrote:

• We're Jack and Annie. We come in peace from America. Who are you?

Jack handed the notebook and his pencil to the moon man. They looked tiny in his big hands.

The moon man looked down at the message. He looked at the tiny pencil. Then he turned the notebook over.

Jack and Annie watched as the moon man put the pencil to the paper. He was writing something very carefully.

Finally he gave the notebook back to Jack.

Jack and Annie stared at the marks.

"Stars," said Annie. "He drew stars."

"Maybe it's a space map," said Jack.

"Space map?" said Annie. "Hey, Jack, *map* starts with M!"

"Oh, wow," said Jack. "This must be the fourth M thing!"

"Let's ask him what his map means," said Annie. She turned around.

"We'll never know now," she said.

"Why?" Jack looked up from the map.

"That's why." Annie pointed. The moon man was flying over the mountains.

"Thanks!" Annie cried.

8

One Star to Another

"Who *was* that guy?" said Jack. "What does his map mean?"

"I don't know," said Annie. "But let's see if it works."

Jack took a deep breath. "Yeah, we'd better hurry back. I think I'm running out of air. It feels harder to breathe."

"For me, too," said Annie.

"Go slow. Don't breathe too much," said Jack.

He and Annie took long, floating steps

toward the moon base. Jack held his breath as if he were underwater.

By the time they got to the white dome, he was ready to burst.

Annie pushed a button beside the huge door. It slid open. They hurried into the air-lock. The door closed behind them and the door to the hallway opened.

Jack opened the visor of his helmet. He took a long, deep breath—and let it out. "Ahhhh!"

"Let's get out of these suits," said Annie.

"Good idea." Jack was dying to free his arms and legs.

As they moved clumsily into the spacesuit storeroom, Jack felt heavy again.

He and Annie unlocked each other's helmets, gloves, and boots, and pulled everything off. Then they stepped out of their bulky suits.

"Whew!" Jack said. He took off his glasses and rubbed his eyes.

It was great to be free—even if he no longer felt as light as a feather.

"Hurry! Peanut's waiting!" said Annie.

She led the way down the steps to the bright landing chamber.

"Yay," she said softly.

Jack was relieved to see the tree house still there. Soon they'd be heading home. He couldn't wait.

Jack and Annie crawled through the tree house window.

"We're back, Peanut!" said Annie.

Squeak! Peanut ran to the letter M.

"We missed you!" said Annie. She patted

the mouse's head. "We met a moon man."

"Sorry, Peanut, but you have to move," said Jack. "We have to put the map on the M."

Annie gently lifted the mouse off the M.

Jack tore the star map out of his notebook. He placed it on the M, next to the mammoth bone, the mango, and the moonstone.

He sighed, then sat back on his heels. "Hand me the Pennsylvania book," he said. They needed the Pennsylvania book to get back home.

There was silence.

Jack turned and looked at Annie.

"It's not working, Jack," she said. "The book's not here."

"What?" Was the map the wrong thing?

They looked around the tree house.

"It's definitely not here," said Annie.

"Oh, no." Jack's heart sank. He picked up the star map and stared at it.

Squeak, squeak. Peanut jumped out of Annie's arms and scurried back to the letter M.

"I've got an idea," said Jack. He reached

into his pack and took out his pencil.

"What are you doing?" said Annie.

"You know how you draw a constellation?" said Jack. "You connect all the stars. What happens if we try that?"

He drew a line from one star to another. He kept drawing, until all the stars were connected.

"Let me see," said Annie.

Jack held the paper out so they could both study it.

"It looks like a mouse," said Annie.

"Yeah," said Jack.

"Is there such a thing as a mouse constellation?" said Annie.

"I don't think so..." said Jack.

Squeak.

Annie and Jack looked at Peanut. She was standing on the M.

"Oh, wow. Jack," Annie whispered, "I think I know what the fourth thing is—"

Jack grinned. "Me too," he said. "It's a—"

"*Mouse!*" they said together.

Squeak! Squeak!

"Maybe the spell is—*Moonstone, mango, mammoth bone, mouse!*" said Annie.

Jack touched each M thing in turn as he whispered, "Moonstone, mango, mammoth bone, mouse."

"Let's say it over and over and see what happens," said Annie.

Together, they chanted:

> "*Moonstone, mango,*
> *mammoth bone, mouse.*
> *Moonstone, mango,*
> *mammoth bone, mouse.*"

Suddenly, a bright light filled the tree house.

The light got brighter and brighter and brighter.

The brightness was blinding and whirling.

The air spun with brightness.

Then everything was clear.

Peanut the mouse was gone.

And Morgan le Fay stood before Jack and Annie.

9

Morgan

"Thank you," Morgan said softly. "You have freed me from the magician's spell."

Jack just stared at her.

"*You* were Peanut?" Annie said.

Morgan nodded and smiled.

"Really? You were with us all the time?" said Jack. "On all our missions?"

Morgan nodded again.

"Why did we have to go on this mission to find a mouse?" said Jack. "If you were always with us?"

"To break the spell, we had to be on the moon," said Morgan. "You could have broken it the minute we arrived."

"Oh, that's what Peanut—I mean *you* were trying to say!" said Annie. "We didn't have to leave the moon base at all."

Morgan nodded, smiling.

"But the moon man came along to help us," said Annie. "He drew a constellation of a mouse! Is he a friend of yours?"

Morgan shrugged. "Let's just say we had a little talk. He stopped by the moon base while you were out."

"The same way you had a talk with the ninja master, right?" said Jack. "And the monkey and the sorcerer?"

Morgan nodded. "I always squeaked to the ones who helped you."

"But how did they understand you—a mouse?" said Jack.

Morgan smiled again. "Certain wise ones understand the language of little creatures," she said.

"I bet it was you who turned the pages of the books!" said Annie. "To show us where to go next!"

Morgan nodded.

"But who turned you into a mouse?" said Annie.

Morgan frowned. "A certain person who likes to play tricks on me," she said. "His name is Merlin."

"Merlin!" said Jack. "The greatest magician who ever lived."

Morgan sniffed. "He's not that great," she said. "He doesn't even know I have two brave friends who help me."

"Us?" said Annie shyly.

Morgan nodded. "And I thank you both with all my heart."

"You're welcome," said Jack and Annie.

Morgan handed Annie the Pennsylvania book. "Are you ready to go home now?" she asked.

"Yes!" said Jack and Annie.

Annie pointed to a picture of the Frog Creek woods. "I wish we could go there," she said.

The tree house started to spin.

It spun faster and faster and faster.

Then everything was still.

Absolutely still.

But only for a moment.

10

Earth Life

The midnight woods woke up.

A breeze rustled the leaves.

An owl hooted.

The sounds were soft, but very alive.

Jack opened his eyes. He pushed his glasses into place.

He smiled. Morgan was still with them. He could see her in the moonlight. Her long white hair was shining.

"Morgan, can you and the tree house stay

here?" said Annie. "In Frog Creek?"

"No, I must leave again, I'm afraid," said Morgan. "I've been gone from Camelot for a long time."

She handed Jack his pack. She brushed his cheek. Her hand felt soft and cool.

"A bit of moondust still on you," she said. "Thank you, Jack, for your great love of knowledge."

"You're welcome," said Jack.

Morgan tugged on one of Annie's braids. "And thank you, Annie, for your belief in the impossible."

"You're welcome," said Annie.

"Go home now," said Morgan.

Jack smiled. Home was Earth—that bright, colorful world where everything was alive and always changing.

"Bye, Morgan," said Annie. She started out of the tree house.

Jack looked back at Morgan.

"Will you come back soon?" he said.

"Anything can happen," said Morgan. "The universe is filled with wonders. Isn't it, Jack?"

He smiled and nodded.

"Go now," Morgan said softly.

Jack followed Annie down the rope ladder. He stepped onto the ground.

The wind started to blow.

The tree started to shake.

A loud roar filled Jack's ears. He squeezed his eyes shut. He covered his ears.

Then everything was silent and still.

Jack opened his eyes. The ladder was gone. He looked through the leaves and branches of the giant oak tree. Where the tree house had been was only moonlight now.

"Bye, Morgan," he whispered sadly.

"Bye, Peanut," said Annie.

Jack and Annie stared at the top of the tree for a long moment.

"Ready?" said Annie.

Jack nodded.

They started for home.

The midnight air felt cool and moist. It was filled with the soft sounds of earth life.

Jack and Annie left the Frog Creek woods. They started down their street.

Annie glanced up at the sky. "The moon looks really far away, doesn't it?"

It did, thought Jack. It *was*.

"I wonder how the moon man can be up there all alone," said Annie.

"What do you mean?" said Jack.

"I mean, who helps him put on his space-suit?" said Annie. "Who helps him get up when he falls down?"

"And who is he?" added Jack.

"Who do you think he was?" said Annie.

"He must be a scientist or an astronaut from Earth," said Jack.

"No. I think he's an alien," said Annie, "from another galaxy."

Jack scoffed. "What makes you say that?"

"I just feel it," said Annie.

"Wrong," said Jack. "There's no proof that aliens exist."

"Maybe not now," said Annie. "But don't forget—we were in the future."

"Oh, brother," said Jack.

They crossed their yard and climbed their

back steps. Annie tiptoed inside the house. Jack followed her.

Before he shut the door, he glanced up at the moon.

Was Annie right? he wondered. Could the moon man have come from another galaxy?

Morgan's words came back to him: *The universe is filled with wonders. Isn't it, Jack?*

"Goodnight, moon man," Jack whispered. Then he closed the door.

About the Author

Mary Pope Osborne visits schools all over the country and talks to students about her Magic Tree House books. "Kids are a great help to me," she says. "I always get them to vote on where they think Jack and Annie should go. Lots of kids even write their own Magic Tree House stories and share them with me."

If you'd like to share *your* Magic Tree House ideas with Ms. Osborne, you can write to her at this address:

Mary Pope Osborne
Random House, Inc.
201 East 50th Street
Mail Drop 28-2
New York, NY 10022